D0832862

Pottery and Porcelain

COLLINS NUTSHELL BOOKS

Pottery and Porcelain

L. M. ANGUS-BUTTERWORTH

With Photographs

COLLINS
LONDON AND GLASGOW

GENERAL EDITOR: J. B. FOREMAN, M.A.

First published 1964

William Collins Sons & Co. Ltd., 1964

PRINTED IN GREAT BRITAIN

BY COLLINS CLEAR-TYPE PRESS

Contents

1

WHAT POTTERY AND PORCELAIN ARE MADE FROM

The nature of potter's earth—Some types of clay—Why clay is plastic and sand is not—The changes due to firing—Turning clay into a liquid for slip-casting—China-clay from Cornwall and Devon—How earthenware is made—Piggins and posset pots—Staffordshire stoneware—The difference between soft and hard porcelain—British bone china—Translucent china—The composition of glazes.

Potter's Earth

The ceramic art of pottery takes its derivation from the Greek *keramos*, potter's earth, and to make pottery we have to prepare a mixture of clay or other materials. In early times clay was used by itself because its plastic nature lent itself well to shaping, but now the composition of the body mixture varies greatly according to the kind of product required. Anything that has to meet so many needs as pottery must differ a good deal in the form it takes, so that we have earthenware, stoneware, porcelain and several other types.

There is no sharp distinction between the kinds of pottery, for they merge into each other. We can see that this is inevitable when we consider that it is possible to obtain infinite variation in colour, closeness of texture, or degree of hardness. In general, the softer and coarser grades are made from materials that are most readily available, and are fired only to a comparatively low degree, so that they are economical in cost although suitable for a great many ordinary requirements. The harder and finer grades incorporate rarer materials like bone ash and are taken to a higher firing temperature, though they justify their costliness by meeting various special demands of either a technical or de luxe nature.

It is evident that primitive pottery must have been baked at what would nowadays be regarded as a very low temperature. It is the practice at the present time to take soft earthenware to at least 750°C., stoneware to about 1,200°, and porcelain to about 1,400°. The firing operation is always a compromise, in that the body mixture must be soft and plastic enough to work with, but hard and stiff enough not to collapse or become deformed when subjected to great heat.

Staffordshire made use of the local clays at a very early date, but it was not until the change-over from wood to coal fuel that the district developed as the main centre of pottery manufacture in Britain. Families long associated with the trade, like that of Wedgwood, then came into their own. And although rough brown pottery was being made in Burslem in the 16th century, a great impetus was given to the industry in the Potteries by the introduction of purer clays from Devon and Cornwall in 1715.

Some Types of Clay

Clay may be described as a hydrous silicate of alumina. When found in a very pure state, as in kaolin or china clay, it contains about 47 per cent of silica, 40 per cent of alumina, and 13 per cent of water. Such a clay will burn to a white or pale yellow colour.

The terra-cotta type of clay has a higher proportion of silica in its composition than kaolin, and is therefore strictly a fireclay. In a raw state its colour varies from grey-green to black. When burnt, and the name *terra-cotta* indicates baked earth, it assumes the brownish-orange

8

colour with which we associate it, betraying the presence of iron impurity.

If an article were to be made from raw fireclay we might expect shrinkage to the extent of about an eighth; half this amount on drying, and half on firing. In making terra-cotta objects, therefore, a proportion of "grog" is used. This is the name given to powdered clay which has already been burnt, and in which the shrinkage has, therefore, already taken place. Grog not only limits the shrinkage but stiffens the clay mixture and helps it to keep the form desired. The grinding up of the material to produce the grog saves the use of new clay and is therefore an economy.

Terra-cotta was largely used by the ancient Greeks for their beautiful Tanagra sculptures; by the Etruscans for the decoration on their tombs; and by the della Robbia family in Italy for their charming figures in relief. For any work of this kind, in which the shape is elaborate, the material has to be uniform throughout, as otherwise shrinkage would be unequally distributed, with resulting breakage.

China-Clay

China-clay is a fascinating substance. Its other name is kaolin, from the Chinese *kao*, high, and *ling*, a ridge, the tradition being that this was the name of a mountain from which the material was originally obtained. In Britain china-clay is mined only in Cornwall and Devon, where there are rich deposits. From the mines in St. Austell and the surrounding district the material is supplied in great quantities not only to Staffordshire and other home markets, but overseas to Canada, the United States and elsewhere.

China-clay results from the natural breakdown or decomposition of feldspar, which in turn is one of the main constituents of granite. It can be formed in long periods of geological time either by volcanic action or by surface weathering.

The weathering of the feldspar comes about partly through the action of sun and frost, but more particularly from that of carbonic acid and water. Especially favourable conditions are provided where there is bog or marsh that provides humic acid to quicken the process.

We may distinguish between primary clays and secondary ones. The former are those found where they were formed or close at hand, and contain a comparatively high proportion of impurities. The latter are those that have been carried to new sites by streams. Only very fine particles of the clay will remain in suspension in the water, large grains being left upstream. In consequence, deposits of secondary clays are very fine and pure, this being notable with china-clay. It is interesting to observe what ideal conditions are provided by the interior of Cornwall for the natural processes we have described.

Such a desirable material as china-clay naturally finds many uses. It is used not only in pottery and porcelain, but in fine papers, especially those that are to carry illustrations, and as a base for face powder and other cosmetics. As a commercial product, however, it always contains a little iron as an impurity. This iron would give a cream colour tint, and its effect is therefore neutralised by the addition of a very small amount of cobalt oxide, which results in a balanced white or very pale blue colour.

Why Clay is Plastic and Sand is Not

We can make pots of clay but not of sand. Why is this? The main reason is that clay is plastic to an unrivalled degree, while sand has hardly any of this quality. Even clay is non-plastic when dry, the change taking place when water is added. The plasticity is helped by the minute size

10

of the clay particles. What is really important, however, is the shape of the clay crystals, as shown by the electronic microscope.

The clay crystals are in the form of thin plates, the scale being almost incredibly small. The crystals may be considered as having only two dimensions, in contrast to the three-dimensional lattice formed by silica and most other things. Scientists have been able to show that because of their shape the clay crystals form into continuous layers, between which there is great molecular attraction when water is added. The plasticity of clay comes about because, when water is present as a lubricant, the crystals can slide along the flat surfaces of each other without loss of cohesion.

The Changes Due to Firing

The term pottery implies not only clay that has been shaped but clay that has been fired in the potter's kiln. The distinction is a very real one, for the treatment at a great heat brings about chemical and physical changes in the clay which cause it to become in effect a different material.

Modelling by hand or shaping in the mould is made easy by the plastic nature of the moist clay, but most of the uses of pottery depend upon the strength and rigidity which result from the firing. In other words, it would not matter how well the clay could be manipulated if it could not be hardened later. On the other hand, if clay began by having the characteristics of its burnt state it could not be used. Plasticity is an essential property during manufacture, just as hardness is during use. It is this unique combination of qualities that counts.

How Clay is Prepared for Use

In the old days, when costs were low and life was more leisurely, the main way of preparing clay was by weathering. By this system the clay was turned over periodically with a spade, so that successive layers of it might be exposed to the action of sun, rain and frost.

Now we are in more of a hurry, and have sought the aid of machines to speed up the natural processes. We use pug mills to treat the clay and remove some of the air from it. Then, after it has been calcined, jaw crushers are employed to break up hard lumps. Finally, pan mills or other types of grinding machinery reduce the material to any desired degree of fineness.

When all the raw materials of pottery have been reduced to fine powder in this way they have to be mixed in whatever proportions are necessary for the goods to be made. The mixing can be done in the dry state, or alternatively each ingredient can have water added to turn it into a semi-liquid creamy slip. Manufacturing operations can then proceed.

Turning Clay into a Liquid

It has been found that stiff plastic clay can be turned into liquid slip without any extra water merely by the addition of an alkali such as carbonate of soda or water-glass. Only a small quantity of the alkali, say 2 per cent, is needed to effect this transformation. In point of fact the process is reversable, so that under conditions of careful control a great power over the material has been gained, and the clay can be made liquid or solid at will. This technique has made possible the bulk production of pottery of difficult shapes by the slip-casting process.

Earthenware

This is much the largest pottery group. The raw materials used include ball clay, china clay, feldspar and flint. Of these the ball clay, which comes mainly from Devon and Dorset, is very plastic and helps to give strength after drying; it makes the body easily workable, and a high proportion is therefore used when the earthenware is to be produced rapidly by automatic shaping processes. The china clay helps to give a better colour, as this tends to be made muddy by the ball clay. The chief function of the feldspar is to act as a flux. The flint prevents the body becoming deformed when being dried or fired.

The body constituents of earthenware are not so finely ground as those used in the better types of pottery and this results in a surface which is coarse in texture. A low firing temperature, too, makes the pot dull and porous. These disadvantages can be overcome by coating with transparent glaze, or by dipping in a slip of fine white clay if a smooth opaque finish is desired.

Piggins and Posset Pots
One of the most famous kinds of earthenware is an English product known as Staffordshire slip ware. This was made at Wrotham as early as 1649, and by Thomas Toft at Shilton in 1660. Among the curious pieces that have survived and are now preserved in museums are: piggins, a kind of small pail or bowl decorated with staves and hoops, with one stave prolonged to form a handle; posset pots, a large cup or covered bowl to hold posset, a drink made with milk curdled with wine or ale; and tygs, an old four-handled drinking cup.

Stoneware
What is known as stoneware contains more silica in its composition than ordinary earthenware, and is taken to a higher temperature in the firing. The resulting product has a closeness and hardness which makes it useful for many purposes.

Stoneware was developed in Flanders and Germany in the 16th century. In England the manufacture of salt glazed stoneware was begun at Fulham about 1670 by John Dwight. His product which was very white and dense, soon surpassed that of the German potters.

Among other pioneers were the Ehlers or Elers brothers, who were working between 1688 and 1710. They had a romantic origin, their father being of a noble family in Saxony, while their mother was the daughter of a burgo-master of Amsterdam. They established a factory near Burslem, where they produced an excellent red stoneware. This was made by mixing Staffordshire clays after wash-ing and sifting them—a thing that had not been done before.

Porcelain

This is fired at a very high temperature, and is semi-vitreous in nature. The first kind to be developed was soft porcelain, or *pâte tendre*, which was followed a good deal later by hard porcelain, or *pâte dure*.

Most of the English porcelain was of the soft kind, and consisted of a white clay mixed with a powdered glass frit. Hard paste porcelain is a mixture of china stone and china clay. In a fused state it is so hard that it is almost impossible to mark it with a file.

The relationship between the terms pottery and porcelain merits careful definition. The general term pottery covers any kind of object made from plastic earth. Porcelain, by contrast, is a particular kind of pottery with certain characteristics dependent upon a composition varying only within a given range of materials.

Chinese porcelain combines kaolin and petuntse, which from the geological point of view are the same rock in different stages of disintegration. The former is an infusible white clay, and the latter a fusible white rock, which together give just the properties of whiteness and trans-lucency required.

Bone China

This is a British speciality. The manufacture of bone china originated in Britain, and there has been very little development of this branch of the industry elsewhere. By contrast most of the fine tableware on the Continent is porcelain, which is now seldom made here for that purpose.

Translucent China

In 1960 a new kind of feldspathic china was introduced by the Royal Doulton company. This translucent china was intended as an intermediate product. It has the delicacy of true china in feel and appearance, combining this with toughness and translucency. At the same time it can be sold at little more than the best earthenware, with the result that in the first twelve months more than a million pieces were required.

Glazes

Common or garden plant-pots are a typical example of plain earthenware. In a glazed finish, pottery is given a glassy coating that is usually transparent. A lustre finish, of the kind found in much Greek pottery, has a kind of glossy sheen. An enamelled finish differs from a clear glazed one in that a coating of opaque or coloured glass is used, which hides the base.

Glaze, as the word indicates, is a kind of glass of a soft nature. It is made of constituents that melt at a lower temperature than clay, in order that it will fuse readily on to the pot, and consists of sand or other allied materials, with lead, potash, or borax to act as a flux.

2

HOW POTS ARE MADE

We see how early pottery was made by hand; how the potter's wheel was discovered and improved; and how modern processes like slip-casting were introduced—The importance of glazing is considered, and we notice how pots have to be fired to make them hard before use—We look at the process of turning, and see how jolleys and jiggers help to make pots—The advantages of mass production are noticed, and reference is made to recent ways of economising in manufacture.

How Pots are Made

We may distinguish five basic methods of making pottery. In practice two or more of these are often combined, but to see their characteristic features clearly it is necessary to examine them separately. They may be termed free-hand working or modelling; throwing on the wheel; building-up; moulding or pressing; and slip-casting.

Free-hand Working or Modelling

The most primitive pottery was shaped by hand, the finished articles being left to dry in the sun. Only later was it discovered that by the application of fire, a material as hard as stone could be obtained. Since a single lump of clay was used, the resulting pot could not exceed a moderate size.

At the present day this natural method has two important uses. First there is figure-modelling, sometimes in elaborate groups, for artistic purposes. Secondly, we have the making of prototypes or models for pottery which is afterwards to be multiplied by mould production. Experimental and research work also demands this method.

Dating from perhaps the 3rd or 2nd Millenium B.C., this unglazed grey earthenware vessel shows close similarity in form to the famous gold vase from Mycenae which is in the National Museum at Athens. *By courtesy of the British Museum.*

This group of figures (Han Dynasty, 206 B.C.-A.D. 220) is made of earthenware and was originally covered with a green lead glaze. Because of decomposition, however, the earthenware has assumed a silvery tint.

Throwing on the Wheel

The credit for the discovery of the potter's wheel does not appear to belong to any one nation. Its use was evolved independently in different parts of the world. Although very ancient it came late compared to pottery itself. The elementary form of the "slow wheel," which came before the potter's wheel proper, consisted of a horizontal table mounted on a central pivot, and rotated by the hand of the potter squatting beside it. This invention was a great help in producing circular vessels.

The next stage of development was when in Egypt a larger wheel was introduced which the potter could turn with his foot. This was a considerable improvement, because both his hands were left free for the manipulation of the clay. Not until the 17th century was a system of pulleys invented for working the potter's wheel. A great saving of labour was effected by the application of steam power in the 19th century, followed by electrical power in the 20th century.

If you try to use a potter's wheel without experience, it soon becomes evident that a great deal of practice is needed to have any success, and that to become expert requires a high degree of skill. As the disc spins rapidly, movement is imparted also to the wet clay. The rotary movement tends to fling the clay outwards, and control has to be exercised through the hands of the potter, who, while working at the wheel, is called a "thrower."

In shaping the clay the thrower works from the base upwards. The clay seems to become alive as it is forced up or down, and opened out or closed in, all at high speed. In the hands of the novice only an unbalanced, inelegant shape may emerge, but the trained craftsman will form with ease a vase or other vessel whose graceful symmetry about its vertical axis reveals the rotary power in which it originated.

Building-up

The three main sub-divisions of this system are kneading, coiling and ringing. *Kneading* consists of building-up the wall of a vessel by working-in sausage-shaped slabs of damp clay. The top of the wall, which in this way is gradually caused to grow upwards, must also be kept moist during operations. *Coiling*, the idea of which is probably borrowed from the similar style of basketwork, is done by winding ropes of clay in a continuous spiral. *Ringing* is like the last named but flat rings placed upon each other take the place of the spiral.

Moulding or Pressing

Through the centuries the methods of moulding pottery have been subject to gradual change and improvement. Even in primitive times considerable ingenuity was shown in finding means of moulding. For example, moulds were formed by preparing in the ground hollows of the right size and shape, or by making a basket framework. Advances were made in other materials, including the handy and convenient hard-baked clay, the difficult but permanent stone, and the adaptable and versatile plaster-of-paris.

It will be evident that by pressing various sections of an object, and joining them together, more elaborate shapes can be made than could be moulded in one operation. The parts of such a vessel can be joined by a suitable mixture of liquid clay known as "slip," the process being termed "luting with slip."

Slip-casting

The interesting and ingenious process of casting pottery is comparatively modern and still has possibilities that have not been fully explored. The "slip" or liquid clay is poured into a mould made in two or more sections. Much depends upon the clay mixture being of exactly the right composition for the particular circumstances ruling at the time of manufacture, so that some of the problems involved are essentially chemical ones. For special purposes, too, electro-casting represents a new technique which, although showing great promise for the future, is still in its infancy.

Time is allowed for drying, a process which is helped by the mould being made of porous plaster that absorbs water, and also by heating. When the object is sufficiently dry it can be released by taking apart the sections of the mould.

Which comes first, the mould or the piece of pottery made from it? Surprisingly it is normally the pot itself. A figure subject or an ornamental article is first modelled free-hand. The cost of repeating original work by hand would be prohibitive, so moulds are made from approved specimens, and then by casting the figure or other object can be multiplied many times over at a low cost.

Glazing

Much of the beauty and usefulness of pottery would be lost if it were not glazed. The glaze, which is essentially a coating of glass, makes it easy to clean and prevents the contents contaminating the clay, which before glazing is naturally porous. Various methods of glazing have been tried. Common salt was once much used for what was known as salt-glazing. When fired the sodium fused with the silica in the pots to form a glaze, but in the process injurious chlorine gas was given off.

Safe glazes are now in general use. A frit or glass is formed from silica and alkali, with lead or borax, and is ground to powder. The frit is mixed with water to form a liquid which can be sprayed on to the pottery, or into which the pots can be dipped. Coloured or opaque white slip is also applied in this way.

Originally, glazes were applied to raw or unfired pots, and must therefore have been of a comparatively soft nature. In the East porcelain is still glazed in this state and, as it is hard, can withstand the treatment successfully with certain limitations as regards the composition of the glaze. In the West much more reliable glazes are obtained by firing the ware before glazing. In the biscuit state the pottery is still quite absorbent enough to take the glaze well.

One important practical use of the glaze coating on pottery is to enable it to hold liquids which would otherwise seep through the porous clay. This was a problem that primitive potters were unable to solve. Their pots had to be fired in the open, usually by means of brushwood and dried grass, and the heat was not sufficient to fire a true glaze properly. In any case, this kind of crude firing was so inefficient that, besides a fair proportion of the ware being directly broken in the process, many pieces were very unevenly baked. In the circumstances it is not surprising to find that for water vessels and the like, primitive people often use varnishes made of gums and resins as an alternative to glazing.

Turning

Mankind is constantly seeking fresh ways of obtaining greater command over his materials, and to do this new processes are introduced or old ones elaborated. The potter, for example, is now seldom content to let a piece of pottery dry in the form in which it was originally made. When the pot has become what he calls "leather dry," that is to say hard enough to keep its form but soft enough to be worked upon easily, it is removed from the mould. Then if it is of symmetrical shape it is mounted on a lathe and a variety of things are done to it.

The "turner," or lathe operator, by means of a cutting tool can greatly reduce the wall thickness, a very necessary operation for some types of ware, because there are strict minima for the thickness at earlier stages. Or again the turner can polish the pot on the lathe.

Jolleys and Jiggers

Recent times have not been kind to the craftsman. In the pottery industry the thrower and turner, upon whom so much used to depend, tend to be superseded by mechanical equipment. These skilled workers still play their very important part in the artistic and semi-amateur section of the trade, which provides an outlet for those who have the impulse to create fine craftmanship as well as for those who wish to have in their homes pots of individual beauty and distinction. In the main, however, the machine operator has attained a dominant position and is responsible for the bulk of output. There is nothing to regret in this transition to mass-production, so long as it is associated with good design.

In place of the thrower and turner we now have "jolley" and "jigger" operators. The "jolley" is a convex mould which is placed upon the wheel for shaping the inside of plates, dishes and other shallow articles. As this device is convex, the plates and other articles are made upside down. The "jigger" is a hollow mould used for the manufacture of cups, bowls and other relatively deep articles. The necessary amount of clay is placed in the rotating mould, and is stamped into shape by a plunger. Other associated aids to production are the "profile" and "templet," used for shaping and gauging the ware.

Automatic Mass Production

In the United States standardisation has been developed to such an extent that it is possible to have bulk production by automatic pottery machines. Dr. Ernst Rosenthal mentions, for example, one of the largest jolleying machines made by the Miller Pottery Engineering Co. On this machine a dozen pieces of hollow-ware or flat-ware, such as cups, saucers, plates, bowls or fruit dishes, are produced at each revolution of the main shaft, and as the shaft rotates twenty times a minute the production is 345,600 jollied porcelain pieces a day. It is estimated that the machine does the work of 180 operatives in one shift, or 720 operatives in a four-shift day.

Such speedy methods of manufacture make a considerable contribution to a high standard of living. Excluding the very limited output of real pottery artists, it is true to say that where hand-making survives comparatively few people can enjoy the product because of the cost, whereas the machine brings it within reach of everybody.

Firing

A characteristic feature of the landscape of the Potteries used to be the tall kilns used for firing the ware, consisting of a cone bellied at the base but tapering at the top. These traditional round kilns are now giving place rapidly to modern mechanised equipment.

The firing of pottery is an extremely important process, and is repeated two or three times according to requirements. After making, the pots even when dried are still in a "green" or raw state and have to be hardened by firing. Following this first firing, the pots, now known as "biscuit" ware, may have an underglazed decoration applied and may then be glazed and fired to make the whole permanent. Even after simple glazing it is necessary to fire in order to fuse the glaze to the pot. Sometimes, too, there is overglaze decoration which again demands its own firing.

When the traditional type of kiln is used for the firing the green pots are placed in fireclay boxes known as "saggars," a word said to be a corrupted form of "safeguard." Movement of the ware inside the saggars is prevented by projecting arms or brackets called "stilts" or "spurs." These arms also ensure that there is space round the pots which will enable the heat to be fairly evenly distributed. The saggars are piled upon each other to form "bungs" and are placed between the flues inside the kiln.

The periodic or discontinuous cone kilns are slow and wasteful. The first firing may take as long as 60 hours, and before the ware can be removed the kiln must be allowed to cool for another 48 hours. These kilns are coal fired.

Today continuous tunnel kilns are being more and more used. These are fired by oil, gas or electricity. The pottery is loaded upon low trucks which pass slowly through the carefully regulated heat of the tunnel. When the pieces emerge they are baked to exactly the right degree.

Modern Kilns

The high cost of fuel makes it vitally necessary for the closest attention to be paid to economical methods of heat-treatment in pottery manufacture. Great changes have taken place in the design of tunnel kilns in recent years, and much higher efficiency has been obtained.

Uniform heating is important and precautions are taken to ensure that every piece of pottery is heated to the same extent. By suitable arrangements of the burners, thermal efficiency has been much improved. As a result it has become possible to reduce the length of the tunnel and to speed up the firing cycle. In addition a large increase in output as well as a marked improvement in the quality of the ware, and a further saving in fuel has been obtained by attention to good insulation.

Economies in Manufacture

Every manufacturer is constantly seeking to make a better

product at a lower price. The problems involved are very complex, and how they are solved depends upon circumstances. In general, however, certain principles on which recent advances have been made can be noted. One is that, as labour becomes rapidly more expensive, there is greater and greater advantage in mechanisation, hence the ingenuity of the ceramic engineer is increasingly in demand. Another is that accuracy of control becomes more and more advantageous, so that it is becoming increasingly common for tunnel kilns for enamelling or decorating, or for on-glaze firing, to be electrically heated. Much thought has been given by the kiln designer to means of preventing glaze from being attacked by sulphur dioxide or other products of combustion. In one direction or another progress is always being made.

3

THE SHAPE OF POTS

What constitutes a good clay shape—Beauty in pottery and the part played by form, function and fashion—The English idiom and the shape of Wedgwood ware—Modelling porcelain—" Won't you stay for a cup of tea? "—How the design of cups, saucers, teapots and coffee pots has developed—The sound tradition upon which the design of our pottery is based—The effect of bulk production on design.

Good Clay Shapes

Clay lends itself to forming in certain ways, so we can make many shapes in clay that would not be suitable for glass, silver or wood. It is the function of the artist, the craftsman and the manufacturer to understand their medium and preserve its integrity. Much pottery is based on the globe shape, mainly because anything round is also very strong, whereas sharp angles are apt to develop cracks in the firing during manufacture and to give trouble when the pot is in use.

Pottery which is poorly designed is a liability. Not only is it a source of nervous irritation and exasperation, but of direct expense. If, through bad design, a lid does not fit well, we find that sooner or later it has one fall too many and gets broken. When a spout or a handle, or even an odd sharp corner, projects in an awkward way, it will not be long before it is knocked off. If we buy a vase to hold flowers, and find that they topple out, we may well decide not to use it, so that it becomes a piece of lumber and eventually finds its way to a jumble sale. The reverse is equally true, so that if pottery is well designed and of good

25

shape it is a pleasure to use, and has a longer life in service.

Beauty in Pottery
What is beauty of form in pottery, or for that matter of decoration? Are there absolute standards? Some say that it all lies in the eye of the beholder, that one design is as good as another, and that it is up to each of us to make a personal choice. Circumstances vary greatly, for the ideas of one generation differ from those of the next; there are marked national preferences, and so on. Nevertheless, a proportion of the ceramics made achieves such excellence that there is general agreement about it. Some Chinese porcelain, for example, regarded at the time it was made as a supreme manifestation of this art, has fully maintained its reputation during the many centuries through which it has survived, so that to-day we appreciate its breath-taking beauty as keenly as the mandarin who owned it a thousand years ago.

It may be that any product of art must also be the product of emotion. The Chinese had such deep feeling about ceramic art that upon occasion murder was committed to obtain possession of a piece of porcelain. By contrast much Greek pottery of the classical period seems coldly intellectual in character. As in the case of their architectural triumphs, but unlike their finest sculpture, much depended upon mathematical calculations. The curves are geometrically accurate, but in consequence lack inspiration. The form or outline is pleasing and graceful in most cases, but is very limited in its emotional appeal.

Form, Function and Fashion
The shape of much early pottery was excellent because the attention of the potter was directed upon form and function rather than fashion. His aim was to make a sound, strong vessel that was well fitted for its purpose.

Beauty often resulted, but as a bye-product. Only later came the unworthy desire to distort and exaggerate, so that truth was lost. In particular, ornaments on pottery have sometimes almost lost touch with sanity in toadying to some passing fashion.

If you were to visit a prosperous farm you might often find a great contrast between the best parlour and the kitchen. The sitting-room might be cluttered up with odd-ments of ornamental pottery and the like, which have no artistic merit and have now become even unfashionable. The kitchen, being the real living-room of the farmer and his family, might have pottery which, though unpre-tentious, is thoroughly pleasing to the eye because it is so well designed for its intended use. For too long beauty and utility were regarded as quite separate things, whereas we are now learning how close is the relationship between the two, and how happily they can be combined.

The English Idiom in Pottery

A national style in pottery first became evident in medieval times. Although pitchers and other water vessels of the 13th and 14th centuries may be termed peasant pottery, lacking as they did precision of shape, they do show that the potter had a masterly sense of proportion. This earthenware, while sturdy and to some extent lacking in refinement, used clay just in accordance with its natural properties.

The sound principles thus established were well main-tained when developments took place later. With rising prosperity in the country under the Tudors, neater and smaller pieces, many of new shapes, became prevalent. There was clearly no lack of vitality in the shaping of the tygs, the cylindrical mugs with hoops, the candle-brackets, the flat pilgrim bottles and the other things which now became common.

The Shape of Wedgwood Ware

Probably no man did as much as Wedgwood in advancing pottery manufacture, and the shape was frequently affected by his activities. Through his keen interest in ceramic materials he was able to develop, about 1775, a valuable forerunner of true porcelain. This stoneware was exceptionally fine-grained and hard, so that it could be used for the most delicate relief work and for other shapes not previously attempted. A piece made from it that is now in the Victoria and Albert Museum, a dish with a twelve-sided scalloped edge, shows the elegance that could be achieved in this medium.

The Modelling of Porcelain

Porcelain ornamental pieces often charm us by a certain irresponsible playfulness in the modelling, made possible and indeed encouraged by the nature of the material. The form of Chelsea china, for instance, can be delightfully audacious, especially in the wonderful period from 1750. The appeal is all the stronger because, side by side with objects showing Meissen or other influences, we get pieces which are altogether English, revealing this not only in the execution of the figures themselves, but also in the rhythmic build-up of such subsidiary features as the branches of trees or the plumage of birds. The modellers were often, in fact, artists of great skill and delicacy, glorying in the response of a medium so perfect for their purpose.

A Dish of Tay

The kindly invitation: 'Won't you stay for a cup of tea?" can never have been heard in England in the reign of Elizabeth the first. Cups and saucers, now found here in the poorest homes, did not exist in their present form, nor anything that resembled a teapot. Thus, we have some of the very commonest articles of pottery, which are also among the most distinctive in shape, that were simply not known to our Tudor ancestors. How has this remarkable change come about?

Tea has been drunk in England for about three hundred years. In September, 1660, Pepys wrote in his famous Diary: " I did send for a cup of tea, a China drink, of which I have never drank before." The habit spread, and two years later he noted: " Home, and there find my wife making of tea, a drink which Mr. Pelling the Pothicary tells her it is good for her cold." The drinking of tea has had an important influence on the pottery industry. The growth of consumption was very striking, as the following figures show:

Year	lb.
1678	4,713
1725	370,323
1775	5,648,000
1801	23,730,150
1850	51,000,000
1901	255,824,617
1950	415,000,000

The first tea came from China, and very soon enterprising Chinese merchants began to send with the tea small amounts of another product for which their nation was famous, namely porcelain, and this included some of the little bowls that they themselves used for tea-drinking.

To begin with, tea-drinking was a fashionable pastime, and in country houses in the 18th century a room was sometimes set apart for the purpose and was decorated in Chinese style. Elegant and delicate oriental porcelain fitted perfectly into such aristocratic surroundings. A new standard was set, and when the drinking of tea spread to a larger section of the population there was a demand for the same kind of "china" that had become established in the homes of society. The coarse pottery that had previously been used for other purposes was no longer acceptable.

Very soon we became as fond of a cup of tea as the people of the Orient, but their habits were not ours. Their teacups never had handles, so that we may wonder how they managed to avoid scalding themselves. In the West the teacup with a handle was soon invented, and the saucer is also a European idea. It is our tea-drinking habit that has done more than anything else to create a huge demand for pottery, because most people seem to use teacups two or three times a day.

Cuppas and Teacups

Have you ever thought about the shape of a cup? The old Roman metal "cuppa," used for something rather stronger than tea (we still speak of a man being "in his cups"), normally had a stem and a foot like the silver cups given to-day as sports prizes. To consider a teacup we see that as a rule it narrows towards the base, perhaps to leave room on the saucer for the teaspoon. It is therefore unlike the coffee-cup, which has a plain cylindrical shape. Most teacups are well proportioned, but a few are made extra wide and shallow, allowing the tea to cool too quickly.

It was natural at an early date to make cup and saucer match both in shape and decoration. What came later was the idea, borrowed from the Continent, of matching up the teapot, the milk-jug and the sugar basin as well. Some shapes are appropriate for each piece in the teaset, but in others a design that appears reasonable in a teacup gives an extraordinary looking teapot.

Saucers

The saucer originally had nothing to do with the teacup, being a dish for salt or sauce. Even now the name is applied to a variety of shallow dishes, but is most commonly used for those placed under tea or coffee cups. As regards the latter purpose the saucer was intended to protect fine furniture from the heat of the cups or the drips from it. In less elegant circles the tea was sometimes drunk from the saucer.

No Sugar or Cream

By drinking their tea neat the Chinese gained the full advantage of its refreshing properties, and did not destroy any of its delicate aroma. Yet they really had no option, for in their case sugar and cream were not available. We came to have a higher standard of living, so that with us a need arose for cream jugs and sugar basins. Nowadays, alas, the cream jug has given place to the humbler milk jug.

Teapots and Coffee Pots

Our first teapots were copies from Chinese models. The best balance is attained with the usual shape in which the spout is directly opposite the handle. For a full-sized teapot this is probably the only practical arrangement, but for small ones used for breakfast in bed or for invalids the spout is sometimes put at right-angles to the handle. Most teapots are rather squat in design.

Coffee—the word is of Turkish derivation—was unknown in ancient China. The shape of coffee pots was copied from silverware. The early models were a fairly tall and elegant version of an elongated pear shape. The spout sprang from near the base and was long and slender, appropriate in the silver that had once been used, but too fragile in porcelain. Now we usually have a short spout

31

at the top of the coffee pot, which minimises breakage and forms a pleasing contrast to the longer spout still used in teapots.

A Sound Tradition

The design of pottery in Britain is based on a sound tradition. On the Continent the trade often depended upon royal or noble patronage for its development, and some of the results were decidedly curious and eccentric. Here we have a more practical outlook, and accordingly our household pottery has usually been designed concentrating more on service than ornament. Incidentally pots made with such modest aims were frequently pleasing and comely in appearance, so that we managed to get the best of both worlds.

It is very interesting to trace the causes which led to British pottery occupying a place of very high esteem in the continental markets. As pioneers in the industrial field we both created a large middle-class and provided well for it. On the Continent class distinction was always sharper. When a middle-class did appear, later than in Britain, it showed keen appreciation of some of our commoner kinds of pottery, which were designed for hard wear in sensible practical shapes.

How Bulk Production Affects Design

Mass production has a far reaching influence on the design of pottery. In the old handicraft days an almost infinite variety of shape was found. At the present time, especially in the United States, the big producers have been obliged to have a very high degree of standardisation. Uniformity is not, of course, the enemy of good design, but it does discourage frequent changes of shape and pattern.

It is evident that if a really wide market is to be reached bulk manufacture must be organised on a scale involving

The beautiful brush-work of the potters of the Sung Dynasty (A.D. 960-1279) is obvious on this porcelain vase which stands about 14 inches high. *By courtesy of the Victoria and Albert Museum.*

Made of porcelain, this German (Nymphenburg) coffee-pot and cover dates from the 18th century. It is 7⅝ inches high and the flowers on it are hand painted in colour. *By courtesy of the Victoria and Albert Museum.*

heavy investment of capital. Items of plant like machinery and moulds are very costly when planning is on these lines. For the manufacturing operations to be efficient every detail must be under rigid control, so that the clay or porcelain mixtures are always the same; sizes and shapes are strictly uniform; the colours of the patterns are applied in perfect register, and so on. Although we seldom spare it a thought, it is a tremendous human achievement to turn out many millions of excellent pieces of pottery at high speed and low cost.

The large-scale producer takes great care to see that the design and shape of the pots he makes are what the purchasing public wants, for if he did not his losses would be heavy. It has been suggested that any kind of standard pottery restricts the choice of the housewife. There are, however, solid advantages to be set against any limitations of this kind, for example, repeat orders can be sent out promptly, so that existing sets of favourite patterns can be matched when breakage occurs.

4

WAYS OF DECORATING POTTERY

Primitive incised decoration—The contribution of different nations to artistic pottery—A Chinese conception of diabolical decoration —How colour is applied—The development of relief decoration— Wedgwood's Jasper Ware—Pottery decoration in the 18th century —The effects of the Industrial Revolution—The bane of painted pottery—Transfer printing and its application to colours—Preferences in pottery decoration—Modern trends: Picasso as peasant potter.

Primitive Incised Decoration

The instinct to decorate things must be nearly as old as mankind itself. At first decoration was naturalistic, but conventional geometrical designs are also found at a very early epoch. Even in the earlier or ruder Stone Age, pottery was roughly scratched with a pointed stick or bone. In the Bronze Age the patterns became more elaborate, with bands of dots and chevrons. Well-trained and talented artists made their appearance at a surprisingly early period, and incised decoration, in more sophisticated forms, has continued in use to the present day.

National Contributions to Art

The different nations have each made their rich contribution to the art of history of pottery. The supremely good work of the Chinese potters will be considered in detail later. The Greeks excelled in formal patterns that reflected their intellectual interests. The Persians were more interested in colour than form, and evolved many enchanting decorations for their pottery, in which delicate shades of blue, turquoise and other colours were interwoven in subtle and intricate ways. The Italians, having worked out a white enamel of particular excellence, found that this provided an ideal background for vivid colour schemes in blue, orange and yellow. Their majolica ware, inspired to some extent by the earlier products of the Spanish Moors, was decorated in a manner that was cheerfully bold and gaudy, while at the same time artistically successful.

Other races of mankind in many parts of the world, in recent times or more remote ages, have had their own distinctive achievements in ceramics. One curious feature is that while potters have steadily acquired greater technical control over their material and processes, this has not been the case to nearly the same extent with decoration. The best artistic examples of ancient pottery reached an extraordinarily high level. Whether or not the individual or the nation excels in the artistic field seems to depend upon a natural gift that cannot be predicted.

Diabolical Decoration

The history of technical discoveries in connection with pottery decoration is full of curious incidents. Arnold Silcock mentions how the Sung potters learnt something that greatly extended their range of colours. They were using copper to give a grey-blue or lavender glaze. By accident a jet of smoke in the kiln sometimes caused a patch on a pot to turn red.

Imagine the horror of the superstitious Chinese potters when they saw their wares marked by what they believed to be mysterious splashes of blood. Evidently a devil had taken up his abode in the kiln. The only safe course appeared to be a pull down the kiln and destroy the porcelain. But familiarity breeds contempt, and when the same thing had happened a number of times a certain amount of confidence returned, and gradually what caused the new colour came to be understood and controlled.

And so, by experiment, a whole range of wonderful fresh colours was developed, including such variants of the original as crushed strawberry, sealing-wax red, and the beautiful *sang-de-boeuf*. Nevertheless, in a period when the true nature of chemical changes were unknown, fear remained, and as late as the 12th century a writer declares that the red splashes occur "when the planet Mars approaches its greatest brightness," and that "then things happen magically and contrary to the usual order."

Baking in the Ashes

One of the methods of obtaining colour is by regulating the heat at which the ware is fired. Thus if a clay is heated moderately a pink colour is obtained, which with greater heat becomes a deep red, and under intense heat a brownish-red. By cutting off the supply of oxygen during the firing, black and grey colours can be obtained. In this way the ancient Egyptians made vases with a blood-red body and a rich lustrous black rim. Their method was to place the rim or mouth in the coals of the fire, so that the air could not get to it, and this part of the vase was accordingly baked in the ashes.

How Colour is Applied

Only mineral colours can be used for decorating pottery, as any other kind would be lost in the firing. A feature which is of great help to the potter is that some of the best-known mineral oxides yield different colours according to the heat of the kiln and the supply of oxygen. Thus under oxidising conditions, with oxygen in excess of carbon, rich reds and browns can be obtained from iron, while with the opposite conditions, in what is known as a reducing fire, greens and greys are obtained. In the same way copper oxide gives its own characteristic reds and greens.

It is possible to apply colours to pottery in a variety of ways. In under-glaze painting the pot is first decorated and then receives a top coating of transparent glaze. The more common method nowadays is to do the work in a number of stages. To begin with, the pot is glazed and fired to a high temperature. Then the decoration is applied, using colours mixed with powdered glass. Finally, the pot is again fired, but this time only to a heat sufficient to fuse the colour to the background.

Relief Decoration

This pleasant form of embellishment was developed in the 18th century and enjoyed a great vogue. The designs were frequently well adapted to the shape of the pots that carried them, and were skilfully and discreetly executed. The subjects shown included foliage, either natural or conventional; female figures in classical costume, sometimes playing lyres; hunting scenes with lively-looking hounds and horses; and cherubs enjoying themselves in a number of unlikely and fanciful ways. Bas-relief was often applied to jugs, mugs and other pottery intended for use, although the wisdom of sticking ivy leaves round the rim of a teacup may be doubted.

The elements of decoration with bas-relief are simple. The figures or foliage are made in a shallow pitcher mould, and when removed from this are placed upon the ware that has already been prepared. The relief work is often white, and is applied to a dark brown or blue background, so that the detail shows up well because of the contrast.

Various leading potters used exactly the same relief decoration. This is because there were master modellers who supplied the trade. This was a natural division of labour, enabling the potter to concentrate upon making good pots, while the man with artistic inclinations and ability could devote his energies solely to decoration. Drawings were sometimes prepared in advance by the modeller and submitted to the potter for approval before the work was carried out.

Jasper Ware

The Jasper ware made by Wedgwood, when first produced in 1775, was of solid colour throughout. Two years later a long series of experiments led to the development of a dipping process, which coloured only the surface but was cheaper. In this Wedgwood showed himself an apt follower of Whieldon, who devoted a good deal of attention to finding ways of disguising the basic texture of clay. By mixing metallic oxides Wedgwood was able to obtain by the dipping process black, blue, lilac, olive, pink, sage-green and yellow.

The 18th Century

The 18th century was in many ways a great century, not least in the arts, but before its close powerful influences were at work which were to cause far-reaching changes not only in England but on the Continent. The main cause was the Industrial Revolution, though this was not the whole story. Napoleon, for example, was very much a villain of the piece as an art patron during the years when he was at the height of his powers.

When things were made by hand, craftsmanship was widely understood and appreciated. Many things, like good pots, were hard to make and were scarce and expensive. Once acquired, therefore, it was natural for them to be cherished for long periods. A proportion of bad work was produced, but compared with what came immediately afterwards, pottery was simple and good, with decoration that was restrained and delicate. Tradition played its part in maintaining standards.

In France the record was not good before Napoleon, but he made things much worse. A self-made man, he was the heir to no tradition. At his Court he set himself to advertise his power and position in a self-conscious way. The old love of abstract beauty, which the Chinese had so carefully cultivated in their porcelain, did not exist for him. Sèvres was made to produce vases and *jardinières* of enormous size, that were gaudily painted in the worst possible taste.

The Industrial Revolution

The same tendency was evident in England, and became most strongly marked in the Victorian era. The Industrial Revolution cheapened production and at the same time made people richer. The great middle-class rose by its own efforts from the ranks of those who had suffered grim poverty. Improved methods of manufacture gave this new class possessions on an unprecedented scale.

Like Napoleon, and for very similar reasons, the Victorian middle-class wanted ostentation. Over-elaborate decoration in pottery was welcomed because it was an indication to friends of the owners' recently acquired prosperity. Rich decoration also gave personal satisfaction to families when they had previously had to put up with the use of very plain things. This outlook was quite welcome too to the manufacturer, who was finding cheap ways of ornamenting, besides being able to hide defects under elaborate patterns.

In the long run the changes in methods of production were, of course, of great benefit to mankind, and form the basis of modern civilised life. For some time, however, there was considerable evidence of crudity, and this had the natural effect of bringing about a reaction in some quarters. The machine was a real benefactor, but many longed for a return to the old days, and so arose the desire to revive handicrafts as the mainstay of commercial production, which led to the work of William Morris and others. We cannot retrace our steps in this way, nor would it be a good thing if it were possible, but the sincere men who attempted it could not foresee future developments.

The Bane of Painted Pottery

It is possible, but very undesirable, to put a landscape painting round the belly of an urn or on the flat central part of a plate. Most of the results of this ill practice have been singularly unpleasant. The pictures nearly always seem very much out of place, besides being artistic failures. What a curious idea, anyhow, to eat one's dinner off a water-colour painting.

Landscape painting on pottery became so much employed that a number of easel painters turned their attention to this profitable sideline. The compositions were conventional and lacking in vitality. Worse still, the colours were offensively garish or so overladen as to become dull and depressing. This chocolate-box decoration also deteriorated in the firing kiln, so that the product was at its worst when finished.

Landscapes were not the only offenders. One Billingsley of Derby set about flower-painting. What, in theory, could be more attractive than flowers—or more unpleasant in practice? Roses were a favourite line—always pink; always the size of cabbages; and always several shown at once. All " Billingsley Roses " could not be painted by the man himself, and there was really no need, for anyone could be trained in an hour or two to paint them just as badly, so that numerous assistants were engaged to do the soul-destroying work. But while this fashion was at its height other methods were making speedy progress, especially transfer printing in its various forms.

Transfer Printing

The invention of transfer printing and its application to pottery soon after the middle of the 18th century had far-reaching consequences. Given a brown impress of the design the operator could apply enamel colours with much greater speed than had been possible with free-hand painting, so that the product cost less and a wider market was reached. There was, of course, loss of spontaneity, but within a generation or two the transfer had become so firmly established that even free-hand artists were seeking employment on transfer work because their own craft was becoming so rare.

Colour Transfers

Printing in colours was a natural development from the earlier monochrome work. This was done by means of lithographs, a finely-grained slaty limestone being originally used, for which a zinc or aluminium plate was later substituted. Black, brown and especially blue were used in this way as underglaze colours before the end of the 18th century, and shades like mulberry and orange followed early in the 19th century, leading to polychrome printing in time for the Great Exhibition of 1851.

No Bees, Bugs or Butterflies

In the decoration of pottery, consumer likes and dislikes are carefully considered. If you are served with salad on a side dish, and find upon removing the last piece of lettuce that you are faced with a realistic representation of a slug, you may not fully appreciate its artistry just at that moment. It has been found, in fact, that in pots for serving food, "no bees, bugs, butterflies or other insects must appear in the pattern." Bizarre or extreme colour schemes do not sell so well as those that are pleasant to live with.

Picasso as Peasant Potter

In 1950, when Picasso reached the age of 70, he celebrated the anniversary by invading what was to him a new field, that of peasant pottery. When a man of genius, who had been such a vigorous innovator in another sphere, chose to turn to pottery, the impact of his ideas was bound to be violent. His pieces in this medium could hardly be regarded as artistically successful, but they were boldly original. Such a quality is to be treasured, for it is often the most difficult task of the designer to think of anything really new. When completely fresh ground is broken it is bound to serve as an inspiration to some and give impetus to many.

One of the themes which Picasso repeated a number of times was that of a bird-like creature—something like a plump owl with zebra markings—in the shape of a vase. A certain crude humour was achieved which might have been unintentional. Some similar pieces were in the likeness of a woman, with the arms forming the handles, just as the wings do in the case of the bird. The wife of the present writer has seen spouted wine stoups from the Mediterranean area based on the female form, but these are very different in colouring and general conception.

5

CHELSEA AND OTHER CHINA

Making pottery in England with clay bought from the Red Indians
—Porcelain inspired by the Chelsea Physic Garden and Aesop's
Fables—Pottery decorated with gold leaf ground in honey—
Cream-jugs for use with strawberries—How a medical man turned
potter—Blue glaze porcelain—The association between Dragons
and Willow Trees on pottery—The kind of tableware used by the
Prince Regent—Lowestoft cornflowers—Punch-bowls in duck-egg
blue—What makers' marks tell us.

Red Indian Clay at Bow

About 1744 a porcelain works was established at Bow, to
the east of the City of London. The partners were Edward
Heylin, a merchant, and Thomas Fry, an engraver and
portrait painter. This was the earliest known porcelain
factory in the British Isles of whose products good
specimens have survived.

The Bow venture is said to have been started in a glass-
house, and to begin with the materials used were an earth
imported through Plymouth from the Cherokee tribe of
Red Indians, and a glass frit made from sand and potash.
After a few years the Cherokee clay ceased to be imported
because china clay, which was cheaper and better, had been
discovered in Cornwall.

At Bow there was offered a "large assortment of china
for the use of Gentlemen's kitchens, Private families,
Taverns, etc." Some ornamental porcelain was also made.
The things produced were clumsier and generally inferior
to those the Chelsea factory was making about the same
time. It is noticeable how closely oriental models were
copied, although in a crude way, and the works was in fact

described for a time as the New Canton Factory. The Bow establishment closed down about 1765.

Old Chelsea Figures

A small factory for the making of soft-paste porcelain is known to have been working at Chelsea as early as 1745, founded by the Hugenots. The first manager was Charles Gouyn, who was succeeded by Sprimont. The latter had previously been a silversmith in Soho, and the early pieces derived their shape from silverware. Sprimont produced some sumptuous pieces for the table.

For a short period, between 1750 and 1760, some charming ware was made that did much to earn Chelsea its great reputation. The figures and flowers were often inspired by those of the royal factory at Meissen near Dresden. Some of the plants, however, were copied direct from those in the nearby Chelsea Physic Garden. Also shown were some of the beasts from Aesop's Fables. A characteristic of these vintage years was the use of soft colours, with little or no gilding. The figures were on *low* bases, and the trade-mark used was a *red* anchor.

Unfortunately a change for the worse took place. Between 1760 and 1770 the pottery made was of a much lower artistic standard than what had gone before. In this latter period figures were placed on *high* bases, and the trade-mark was a *gold* anchor.

A profitable line that was extensively developed at Chelsea from about 1760 was that of vases and other objects made in imitation of Sèvres ware. The pieces, which often sank to a low level of vulgar bad taste, had the whole surface coloured and gilded except for white panels on which were painted flower or figure compositions.

Although Chelsea porcelain had become deplorable from an artistic point of view, the proprietors evidently had good technical knowledge. Their gilding, for example, became well known. To begin with, says William Burton, who was fully acquainted with the practical side, it was applied in the Chinese manner. Gold leaf was ground in honey and used as a paint, and was afterwards fired until it united with the glaze. Later an advance was made in this method, and a much brighter gilding was obtained. The improved technique consisted of mixing gold with mercury and then grinding finely with a small proportion of readily fusible glass.

This new kind of gilt could be applied thickly, and burnt so hard that it could be safely burnished to extreme brilliance. It was natural to revel in such a facility, and the makers threw discretion to the winds. The pity was that tasteless ostentation was to have a long innings that was not confined to Chelsea.

A large export trade was developed in what were known as "Chelsea Toys." These were small objects often modelled as figures, but designed also for use as scent bottles and the like. In spite of this continued success on the practical side, differences arose among the partners, who in 1770 sold the factory to Duesbury of Derby. Under the new owner development was continued.

Duesbury of Derby

The Derby porcelain factory was founded in 1750, and is a good example of the elements that need to be brought together to establish a business enterprise. To make fine china required finance, practical knowledge and artistic taste. The three men who at Derby "became co-partners in the art of making English china," each contributed one of these things.

The one who provided ready money for the venture was John Heath, a scrivener and moneylender in Derby, who invested £1000, a sum worth much more then than it is now. The practical man, as regards pottery bodies and glazes, was Andrew Planché, who was already occupied as a china-maker in the town. Planché had had continental experience, and is said to have been trained as Dresden. The artistic partner was William Duesbury (1725-86) of Longton in Staffordshire, who was skilled in enamelling and decorating.

Duesbury, who was a good business man as well as an artist, proved to be the stable element in the partnership, and eventually he became the sole proprietor of the factory. In later life he extended his interests so greatly that he came to occupy the premier position in the English porcelain industry. Keeping his headquarters at Derby he bought out a number of rivals.

Strawberry Leaf Cream Jugs

Some white porcelain cream-jugs of Derby make are ornamented with strawberries and their leaves. One such, inscribed " D.1750," is now in the Victoria and Albert Museum. Such objects suggest high summer and the traditional English fare of strawberries and cream. In addition figures of dancers were made here between 1751 and 1753. It seems probable that the figure subjects were made by Andrew Planché.

The Derby Porcelain Manufactory was soon offering a "Great Variety of useful and ornamental Porcelain, after the finest Dresden models." An advertisement of 1758 declared the Derby figures to be "the nearest to Dresden," and showed that the business was prospering by the declaration that: "As with great Care and Expense this Factory is allowed by all judges to exceed any Thing of the kind made in England, and the great demand there is for them, has encouraged the Proprietors to enlarge this Manufactory, and have engaged double the number of Hands they used to employ."

As was usual elsewhere, the Derby factory produced porcelain both for use and ornament. The tableware made there had an agreeable creamy-white base which was tastefully painted. Again, as happened in other places, the first decorative figures made were modelled well and given delicate colouring. After 1760, however, the output was rapidly raised, while the quality of the goods was allowed to decline steeply.

Chelsea-Derby ware had its own characteristics. We find that tableware sold under the joint trade-mark of the two establishments was often decorated with graceful but decadent paintings of classical urns and festoons. Classical themes, and especially funereal urns, were long both fashionable and popular.

After about 1780 the Chelsea-Derby combine was guilty of placing on the market patterns in the most staggering bad taste. Detailed landscapes in bright but unnatural colours competed with huge cabbage-roses and other flowers, all shown in the most wooden way possible. These gaudy displays were varied with flashy "Japan" patterns.

Blue Glaze Porcelain

In the second half of the 18th century two Staffordshire factories, at Longton Hall and New Hall, made their contribution to the history of English porcelain. The former works was established by William Littler in 1752. According to Shaw it was Littler and his brother-in-law, Aaron Wedgwood, who first introduced the use of cobalt in the manufacture of Staffordshire salt-glazed ware. Some of the pieces made at Longton Hall had in fact a bright blue glaze. As with other master potters in those early days, Littler would probably be his own principal modeller.

A Medical Man Turns Potter

Worcester was another early centre of porcelain manufacture. In this case the enterprise sprang from the experiments of two amateurs. The leading part was taken by Dr. John Wall, a wealthy medical man who had long been interested in both porcelain and stained glass. With others he formed a company in 1751, the initial capital being £4,500, representing several times that value to-day.

Among Dr. Wall's partners were W. Davies, an apothecary, whose chemical knowledge would be useful, and Edward Cave, editor of the *Gentleman's Magazine*, who received a return for his investment in the form of advertisements for his journal. Two workmen, Podmore and Lyes, who had helped with the early experimental work and therefore knew some of the trade secrets, were promised gratuities and a small share in the profits, "to ensure their fidelity."

Dr. Wall died in 1776, but the firm continued until 1840, when it was merged in Chamberlain's Worcester Porcelain Factory. Chamberlain himself was employed in his early days at Dr. Wall's factory.

Tableware for the Prince Regent

Robert Chamberlain, the remarkable man who founded the factory bearing his name, began his career at the Wall porcelain works in 1783. Not content to remain in a subordinate position, he branched out on his own six years later. His skill lay in decorating and the method he adopted was to buy plain porcelain from Caughley in Shropshire and decorate it.

Chamberlain rapidly built up a prosperous connection. As soon as he was established sufficiently firmly he decided to advance from merchantry and decorating to manufacture, and here again his enterprise met with success.

Between 1811 and 1816 he evolved an expensive white porcelain that provided an excellent background for rich and minutely elaborate decoration. One of his earliest patrons for this ware was the Prince Regent. The work of decorating this "Regent" porcelain, which was reserved for special services, was taken up by Humphrey Chamberlain, the son of Robert. The son's work is now sought eagerly by collectors.

Dragons and Willow Trees

We saw that Chamberlain, before making his own pottery, bought the plain ware from Caughley in Shropshire for subsequent decoration. The manufacture of porcelain at Caughley began about 1772. The works here deserves fame for having originated two famous patterns—the Willow Pattern and the Broseley Dragon, both originating from Chinese sources. Another point of interest about this factory is that Thomas Minton, who afterwards founded the celebrated Minton Pottery at Stoke-on-Trent, was trained as an engraver here. In 1799 the Caughley Works were acquired by John Rose, who appears to have served his apprenticeship here, but who had risen to become the proprietor of the Coalport China Works.

John Rose built a pottery at Coalport about 1790. The works was on the banks of the Severn, and the site was well chosen, for opposite it a new canal joined the river. This canal had been cut to bring coal to the Severn from the Madeley Wood Collieries, thus giving rise to the unromantic name Coalport at the river junction. Not only, therefore, was cheap fuel available to John Rose, but it proved possible for him to obtain good fireclay for his kilns and saggers from the same source.

Lowestoft Cornflowers

Only brief reference can be made to the minor English porcelain factories of the early period. At Lowestoft in Suffolk a factory was active from 1757 to 1802. Some of the pieces made here were of a modest kind, such as blue-

and-white inkpots and cylindrical mugs. Although intended for uncritical people they are pleasing in their simple decoration of cornflowers and the like. Some of the things that have survived were evidently sold to visitors for use as small presents or souvenirs.

Punch-Bowls in Duck-Egg Blue

At Liverpool, during the latter part of the 18th century, Zachariah Barnes, Richard Chaffers, Samuel Gilbody, Seth Pennington and other worthies were making porcelain in fair quantities. They used no factory marks, and accordingly when collectors have experienced difficulty in identifying their treasures it has often been found convenient to give credit to the Merseyside city. This kind of attribution is all the more natural because Chaffers and other local potters were trained outside their own area, so that their wares have close affinities, for example, with the Worcester tradition.

A Liverpool characteristic that is mentioned by Fisher is a blue which, because of some impurity in the cobalt, has the appearance of being wet and sticky. Another is a pleasant duck-egg blue with a greenish translucency. A favourite product to which such colouring was applied was punch-bowls decorated with pictures of ships in the Dutch style, appropriate enough in a port where so many customers were concerned in one way or another with the sea.

The Change from Soft to Hard Paste

The old English porcelain we have been considering was all of the soft-paste variety. The change to hard-paste porcelain marked the end of an era, and heralded the transition from handicraft methods to modern production.

The first English factory for making true hard-paste porcelain was opened at Plymouth in 1768 by William

Cookworthy. He undertook the manufacture of most kinds of ornamental and domestic pottery, but attempted too much before the nature of the raw materials was fully understood. In consequence he failed in business, and in 1781 sold his patent rights to the New Hall works in Staffordshire.

The making of a superior kind of soft-paste porcelain continued at Coalport, Nantgarw and Swansea. From the beginning of the 19th century, however, Staffordshire, which had already earned a great reputation for the production of earthenware, began to achieve pre-eminence also in the large-scale manufacture of hard-paste porcelain.

Makers' Marks

It has long been the custom to mark pottery and porcelain in some distinctive way, and much can be learnt from these marks. The practice is very like that of placing a hall mark on silver. In pottery the chosen badge or letter is painted or stamped on the bottom of the article. Some of the markings have become famous, for example, the anchor of Chelsea, painted in different colours at different periods, and the capital initial "D" for Derby ware.

The celebrated Crown Derby ware carried a "D" surmounted by a crown, and after the fusion of the Chelsea and Derby porcelain factories a new badge was formed by combining the Chelsea anchor with the Derby "D." It is necessary to add that it is not uncommon for the marks on valuable antiques to be faked on modern reproductions.

6

CHINESE POTTERY AND PORCELAIN

The Place of Ceramics in China—Form and Decoration—Cauldrons for Witches and others—Confucius and Ceramics—Blue-and-White Ware—Celadon Glaze—Colour Glazes—Thin-walled Porcelain—Sung, Ming and Ch'ing Ceramics—The Hill Jars of the Han Dynasty—Tea drinking in the T'ang period—The Great Sung period —The evolution of Porcelain—Buying bowls for Chicken Wine—A Sung Lotus Bowl—Mings and Mongols—Palace Porcelain—Chopstick Saucers and Incense Burners—The Spotted Dogs of Fo and Dragon Fish-Bowls—Apple-green and ox-blood orange decoration on egg-shell China—Japanese Pottery—The Porcelain of Japan—Gold and Scarlet Brocade.

The Place of Ceramics in China

The pre-eminence of the Chinese in ceramics is a reminder that in the history of the nations it has often happened that there has been a magnificent flowering in a particular art. Thus we have the sculpture of the Greeks, the paintings of the Italians, and the music of the Austrians. In China we may say that a new art was created, for nowhere else was the making of ceramics brought to such a height as to be comparable with the traditional great arts like music, painting and architecture.

The kind of faculty to which we have referred is frequently long-continued as well as exclusive. In China the making of ceramics of outstanding merit went on for century after century, keeping pace with and exemplifying the natural evolution of the product. Daughter traditions in pottery were developed in Japan and Korea, and later in Siam, but what was made in these places was never in the same category as regards excellence.

Form and Decoration

At a very early date potters in China seem to have had graceful shape as their main aesthetic objective, for one of them wrote that "Pattern and bright colours detract from the merit of pottery." Form covers a wide field, and from the beginning the Chinese were successful in harmonising such accessories as handles, legs and lids with the body part. Not only were these features well constructed, but they were subordinated so that the conception as a whole had true balance.

One of the secrets of the elegance and beauty which the Chinese achieved in such high degree in their ceramics was the outcome of this restraint in decoration. Good shape in pottery is a subtle and civilised thing, appreciated by the cultured mind, but tending to be overlooked by the multitude. The risk that arises when decoration is used to excess is that, although there may be strong popular appeal, the shape may suffer. If the pot is used mainly as a base for ornament or painting, the form may become debased without anyone being conscious that this has happened. The Chinese were much too wise to make this mistake.

Cauldrons for Witches and Others

Among the primitive Chinese cooking pots made from coarse grey clay were various types of cauldrons. There was the witches' cauldron shape, found here as well as in the West, and another which remained characteristically Chinese. The latter seems to have begun its career simply as a vessel with a pointed base, but afterwards it was elaborated. What was eventually evolved was a tripod cooking pot. In this type of cauldron the three hollow legs, which were just elongated parts of the body, were made to stand sufficiently high to enable a fire to burn underneath. This unique receptacle must have been very difficult to clean, but probably nobody bothered.

Confucius and Ceramics

The habit of burying clay objects with the dead was influenced by the great Chinese philosopher known to the Western world as Confucius (551 to 479 B.C.). In a curious way his moral teachings stimulated the development of the pottery-making craft.

In very early times in China, as in certain other parts of the world, it was the custom for wives, servants and domestic animals to be buried alive with chieftains. We are naturally shocked by a horrid practice of this kind, but the general idea was to provide for the needs of a future life.

By the time of Confucius refining influences had long been at work and changes were due. He used his authority as a great moral thinker to condemn the burial of the wives of emperors and nobles as part of the funeral ceremonies of their husbands. At the same time he was a strong believer in tradition and "saving face," so that he proposed the substitution of pottery statuettes for the human sacrifices. While his ideas were generally acceptable, their adoption took place only gradually. Once the ferment of ideas was operating, however, it quickly extended its scope. As Silcock has remarked in his book on *Chinese Art*, if a clay model of a wife would do, why not clay models of other things?

So with the progress of their civilisation the Chinese came to substitute earthen imitations not only for humans and cattle, but for all kinds of valued household objects. This has enabled us to recover great numbers of fine specimens of ceramic art, for this grave furniture was wrought with much care and skill. It has also brought to modern scholars a flood of knowledge about the mode of life in ancient China, including art, costume and the like.

Before considering some of the products of the different periods in more detail, it may be useful to give a brief summary of their leading characteristics.

No period of Chinese history was more brilliant than that of the T'ang dynasty (A.D. 618-906). China was then perhaps the mightiest empire of the world. Ceramics had not the refinement they were to achieve later, but had a refreshing naturalism. Potters were so skilful that they were able to show movement vividly in their pieces, especially in such subjects as horse and rider or in dancing figures.

Many of the figures recovered from T'ang tombs are large in scale and of superb modelling, so that they form very striking objects. Brilliant colours were used, which originally must have given the pieces a barbaric splendour. Now the paint or enamel is often largely worn away, revealing the hard-baked earthenware underneath, but this gives its own beauty. The usual objects are horses, camels, servants and friendly demons.

The Sung dynasty (960-1279), was a magnificent era. In China during these centuries " The ceramic arts produced those vessels which combined shape and glaze in an unsurpassable harmony."[1]

Another authority says: "With the Sung dynasty we arrive at a period when, from the point of view of form, the potters of no other nation at any time or period have been able to produce anything of comparable quality."[2] This high praise applied not only to pieces for ornament but to those for use, like tea-bowls, wine-cups and flower-pots. The colours have been likened to cherry-red, shades of peach, and to that of the sky after rain.

Under the Ming dynasty (1368-1644), whose capital was first Nanking and afterwards Peking, some baroque

[1] *Chinese Art*, by William Cohn, 1930, p. 7.
[2] *Chinese Art*, by Leigh Ashton and Basil Gray, 1936, p. 182.

features appeared. Artistic effort was concentrated on the decorative element, and porcelain of dazzling perfection was produced.

The Ch'ing or Manchû dynasty (1644-1910), saw in the 17th and 18th centuries what has been described as full-blooded, splendour-loving times. A good tradition had been inherited, but interesting developments were to take place, as in the luscious green tones of the *famille verte* ware (1662-1722), and the blended rose tints of the *famille rose* (1723-35). Finally however, when the days of the dynasty were drawing to a close, and the nation was in decline under the impact of growing Western influence, ceramics too became debased.

Blue-and-White Ware

The celebrated blue-and-white porcelain of China was actively developed under the Ming dynasty. The extent to which regular trade routes were already open is shown by the fact that most of the cobalt used for colouring this ware was imported from Persia. The decoration very often took the handsome form of the dragon and the phoenix, symbolising the Emperor and Empress. It may be mentioned however, that the Chinese had a very wide range in their designs. In the West the Greeks were fascinated for a long period with showing on their pots human figures in action, either in battle scenes or engaged in various sports. In Turkish and Persian ware, on the other hand, religious reasons caused this element to be lacking, and attention was concentrated on geometrical and other abstract patterns. In Chinese ceramics nothing seemed to come amiss in the way of decoration, good use being made of figure subjects, animals both real and imaginary, flowers and foliage, both natural and conventional, and purely abstract designs. For the Chinese to have such versatility shows how advanced they were at a very early date.

At the start blue-and-white ware was something designed for Court and aristocratic use inside China, and the demand for it grew as it came to be realised that here was a product of quite exceptional merit. Although essentially simple, it achieved perfection in its own way. So its fame spread, and under the Ch'ing dynasty export to the West began to take place on a large scale. So blue-and-white bowls became favourite objects with collectors, a fashion which has not changed with the passing of time. It is interesting to see how, in a case like this, artistic taste is the same all over the civilised world, but no doubt this applies only to things of the first rank.

Celadon Glaze

Celadon was the earliest and most famous of the Chinese self-coloured glazes. Its colour was a subtle mixture ranging from grey to sea-green, with sometimes just a suggestion of blue. The European name by which it has become commonly known was taken from Céladon, a popular character on the French stage in the 17th century. The grey-green of his costume was fashionable, and as the colour resembled that of the Chinese porcelain in question, which was also enjoying a vogue at the time, it was natural for the name to be transferred.

The virtue of pieces treated with this kind of glaze lay in the beautiful discreet colouring and in the fine surface texture. Hence much decoration of other kinds was undesirable and, with the usual good taste of the Chinese in aesthetic matters, was restricted to slight ribbing or to low relief, the latter in the form perhaps of lotus flowers and leaves with elegantly trailing stems.

Through the centuries there were many variants of this kind of ware. Reference to one must suffice. In the British Museum there is a specimen of Celadon self-colour glaze dating from the 13th century. The glaze is of a pale blue

57

tint known as clair-de-lune and round the neck, in striking colour contrast, are tear-shaped drops of red resembling sealing wax.

The French have never lost their liking for Oriental porcelain, and in the 18th century spectacular use was made of Celadon ware. Superb examples of the porcelain, usually vases, were provided with magnificent settings of gilt bronze by the bronze workers of Louis XV.

Colour Glazes

We have had occasion to notice the beauties of colour in Chinese porcelain while discussing some of the leading wares of the great periods. Their colour glazes are so attractive and interesting however, that they deserve to be mentioned in a note of their own.

In the Ming dynasty, particularly during the 15th and 16th centuries, two breath-taking colours were developed that were both derived from copper. They were a ruby-crimson and a brilliant apple-green. But just as in other branches of metallurgy there was a move from the use of copper and bronze to that of iron, so in the manufacture of Chinese procelain we find that in the 18th century the use of copper was abandoned and in its place a very pure coral-red glaze was obtained from iron. About the same time the palatte was enriched by the addition of single glazes in elegant shades of sapphire and turquoise-blue.

A vivid insight into Chinese mode of thought in the periods considered is given by the picturesque descriptions they gave to their colour glazes. A green was compared to the plumage of the kingfisher; another delicate shade was said, very accurately, to resemble that of a robin's egg; while deep shades of purple, brown and black were likened to mule's liver and horse's lung.

The colours seem always to have just the right degree of intensity. They are virile as well as delicate, never giving the impression of being faded. Upon occasion, too, the Chinese potter could be exceedingly bold, indulging in colour that is gorgeously rich, but even here there is nothing harsh or ill-conceived, the effect being calculated to a nicety.

Thin-walled Porcelain

The degree of aesthetic maturity reached by the Chinese in their porcelain was remarkable. They became connoisseurs who appreciated and demanded the highest quality in every element in the make-up of the ware. In the first place they found intense pleasure in purity and suavity of form. Perhaps next came their deep understanding of colour in the almost infinite variety of shades which still delight our eyes to-day. Finally came their attention to the matter of thickness.

The maker of porcelain has always been interested in experimenting with thin ware. The composition of porcelain, combined with thinness, gave a gleaming translucency that could not be obtained in any other way. The Sung potters produced a white porcelain of this kind which was very much a luxury article in being extremely delicate and fragile. Under the Mings, too, potters working quite independently made the t'o-t'ai or bodiless porcelain, so called because the walls were of such exquisite fineness that they appeared to be made of glaze alone.

Granted that the Chinese knew how to make this delicate ware, which among other things provided dainty "china" for the use of the Imperial Court, it is a little surprising that for a long time it was not exported. The reason for this does not appear to have been any disinclination or prejudice. Why they sent only coarser ware abroad was probably because their better qualities would not have survived transit over great distances by junk and caravan.

Sung, Ming and Ch'ing Ceramics

The arts of peace and of a civilised mode of life have had a long history in China. In ceramics the Chinese seem to have had a natural gift which was cultivated very early, for they began to excel in this art over two thousand years ago. The chief periods were as follows:

Han Dynasty	206 B.C. to A.D. 220
T'ang	618 to 906
Sung	960 to 1279
Yüan (Mongol)	1280 to 1367
Ming	1368 to 1644
Ch'ing (Manchû-Tartar)	1644 to 1910

(K'ang, 1662 to 1722 was a period in the Ch'ing dynasty)

The Emperor Chêng did much to consolidate China. He not only united a number of the earlier feudal states, but it was he who built the Great Wall of China to keep out the savage nomads of the north. His short-lived dynasty came to an end in 206 B.C., and was succeeded by that of the house of Han. By that time, however, foundations had been laid for vast extensions of power and wealth. In the Han period, which lasted for over four centuries and did not end until A.D. 220, the Chinese empire assumed the form that it was to retain for so long. The first indirect contacts were made with Rome; Buddhism was introduced; and marked progress was made in the arts.

Pottery of Han times has survived mainly because of the practice by the Chinese of the widespread primitive custom of burying objects with the dead for use in their future existence and to comfort their spirits. Among the pottery recovered from Han graves are models of domestic utensils, servants, animals and so on. These are usually of unglazed clay, but are sometimes painted in red, white and black. They constitute a most valuable and fascinating record of contemporary costume and mode of life.

The Hill Jars of the Han Dynasty

In the Han period the makers of pottery had not yet developed a style of their own, being still content to copy the bronze vessels of an earlier age. Common to both bronze and pottery, for example, are the Hill Jars, so named after the Taoist Mountain of Paradise which they bear as part of their decoration. The jars have conical lids, shaped to represent the Isle of the Immortals rising above the waves. On the lower part of the jars there is often lively decoration in the form of a "flying gallop" of bears, deer, tigers or grotesque imaginary creatures.

Of the same period are granary urns that preserve the form of the classic Chinese corn barn. One of the fascinating things about these ancient pieces is the way in which they can illuminate quite a different craft, in this case that of architecture. Although buildings, costumes, etc., may long have been lost, we may still have the good fortune to find a record remaining in another art medium.

Tea Drinking in the T'ang Period

Both in the East and in the West tea-drinking has had a profound effect upon the development of pottery. In China it first became the fashion in the T'ang period, and the custom gradually had an extensive influence in bringing refinement to the pottery used. In spite of improvements, however, it is doubtful if genuine porcelain as we know it was made at this time.

Under the T'ang Emperors a wider range of things were buried with the dead. It became the ideal to provide everything the deceased would need to resume their earthly mode of life in comfort. The pieces of pottery are natural although not unsophisticated. They are simple in a highly civilised way, so that one feels that they were made by pleasant people. Among the small clay models are horses ridden by warriors or ladies of high rank; bulls, camels, sheep, swine and other domestic animals; and fantastic beasts like the gryphon. Figure subjects include musicians and dancers together with many citizens of both sexes and of widely differing occupations.

The Great Sung Period

Under the Sung dynasty China saw the development of a civilisation which in some respects reached a height that has rarely been equalled since. The contemplative, peaceful and intellectual culture that prevailed was specially favourable for art. In the period of over three centuries during which the Sung dynasty held sway the making of ceramics was brought to a pitch of perfection which ever since has earned the admiration of the world.

Chinese pottery and porcelain deserves to occupy a special place in our affections. The finest specimens are incomparably decorative. They have a beauty which seems to be the outcome of pure genius on the part of the makers, and which is extremely difficult to analyse. Thus in shape there will sometimes be subtle curves of flange, body or base that defy mathematical definition, yet are breathtaking examples of inspired craftsmanship.

In our age probably few people regard ceramics as a true art medium. Production in bulk is an industry, while the work of the studio-potter is a craft, but ambitions are usually modest, and there is little challenge to painting and sculpture. In China the position occupied by pottery and porcelain was always more distinguished. Under the Sung dynasty ceramics may well be regarded as the supreme artistic manifestation of the age. No other art then came in the same class either in achievement or in the esteem of connoisseurs.

The full force of exquisite artistry can be felt in Chinese pottery that is perfectly plain except for its gracefully curving lines, though their ware excels equally in colour and texture. And the tradition, having become firmly established, was maintained in various forms for several centuries, earning such a reputation, even in Europe, that the design of much of the early porcelain of the West, like that made at Meissen and Sèvres, was derived largely from Chinese sources.

The Evolution of Porcelain

Just what constitutes true porcelain is quite a complex conception. The Chinese came to recognise certain characteristics as being desirable, especially whiteness, hardness, transparency, and a good ring when struck. When our turn came in the West we had their porcelain to serve as a model, and could therefore make more rapid progress, although in such matters it is never safe to claim that finality has been reached. In the East, however, the problem was the exciting one of advancing slowly towards an unknown goal. It is believed, indeed, that one of the first steps in the right direction was the unintentional result of attempting to imitate jade.

Buying Bowls for Chicken Wine

Chinese porcelain was the object of the utmost devotion on the part of the Court, the families of the mandarins, and those responsible for its manufacture. Ceramic antiques were always held in high esteem, this being in accord with the general Chinese custom of venerating ancient things, but R. L. Hobson tells also of a great price being paid for bowls in Sung porcelain for serving chicken wine, long before they had become true antiques, because they were recognised as objects of supreme beauty and valued accordingly.

A Sung Lotus Bowl

The design of Oriental pottery often relies upon a single bold concept which is carried out with exquisite attention to detail and a sensitive feeling for harmony of form. A stoneware bowl of the Sung dynasty now in the Freer Collection shows these points. The petals of the flower enfold the object, and there are many refinements: the petals are large at the base but become rapidly smaller near the rim, and each has a vertical rib in darker colour. The gradation of petal size gives a sense of balanced stability and the dark ribbing emphasises the strength of the whole conception as an artistic unity. The tip of each petal stands out a little, giving life to the design, and striking a note of authentic naturalness. The outer surface is closely crackled, and is thus provided with an interesting texture.

This use of crackle as an element in decoration is characteristic. A stoneware vase in the Eumorfopoulas Collection, of Sung dynasty, is of the utmost refinement. It is exceedingly well proportioned, avoiding the horrid distortions of which we have so often been guilty in more modern times. The pale colouring is austere, but gains warmth from subtle shades that melt into one another without any sharp definition. The vase is in fact conceived on exceedingly severe lines, and is free from decoration apart from having delicate and widely spaced crackle.

Most forms of decoration tend to take on a machine-like regularity from the repetition of some chosen theme. A crackled surface is graceful because the lines are natural ones. What appears at first sight to be a haphazard pattern will soon be seen to vary only within limits dictated by the degree of heat treatment to which the vase has been subjected. How sensitive is the mind that uses anything so elusive as crackle as a decorative form of elegance.

Painted in enamel colours this porcelain vase and cover was made in Berlin about 1750 and is 16 inches high. *By courtesy of the Victoria and Albert Museum.*

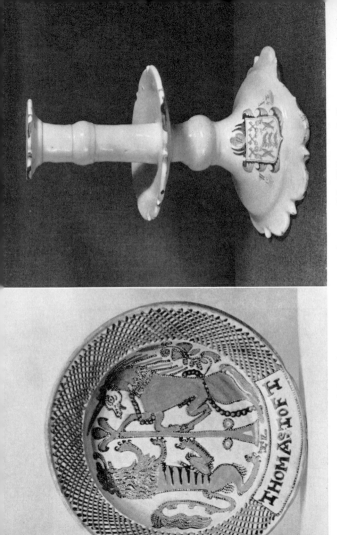

This Staffordshire Slipware dish of the 17th century depicts the Lion and the Unicorn fighting for the

The arms of the Fishmonger's Company are painted in blue on this tin-enamelled earthenware candlestick which is English (Lambeth) dated 1648. By courtesy

Mings and Mongols

Between the great Sung and Ming periods there was a Mongol interlude that lasted for nearly a century. It was in 1368 that the Ming or "radiant" dynasty ousted the Mongols from power. There followed nearly three centuries of peaceful progress, the like of which was unknown in Europe, during which the arts were greatly advanced. Much of the porcelain of this period is of exceptional merit.

Palace Porcelain

The history of the pottery city of Ching-tê Chên is extra-ordinary. This was a very early centre for the production of pottery, and under the protection of Hung Wu (1368-1398), the first Ming emperor, it became the leading place in the world for the manufacture of porcelain. Twenty kilns were then engaged in producing "palace porcelain" for the Imperial household.

Ching-tê Chên grew from being as it were the Royal Dresden factory of China until it became the Staffordshire of the East. Some details of the later career of the establishment are given by Père d'Entrecolles, a missionary of the first part of the 18th century. He says that by his day the city was about four miles round, had 3,000 kilns working, and a population of about a million people all connected in some way or another with the porcelain industry.

The kilns gave the place a characteristic appearance, so that anyone coming down from the surrounding mountains in the evening might think it was on fire. And quite often such a visitor would be right, for the kilns were a real source of danger and fires were not uncommon. In spite of such handicaps, however, a great output was maintained much of which went for export.

Chopstick Saucers and Incense Burners

The porcelain of the latter part of the Ming period included a great range of articles: chopstick saucers, incense burners, perfume boxes, wine cups, betel-nut caskets, fish bowls and gobang boards. The symbols chosen for purposes of decoration on these were often delightful and were also highly imaginative. Thus we have dragons and phoenixes flying through flowers; lions sporting with embroidered balls; the Eight Immortals crossing the ocean, worshipping the god of longevity; lotus flowers and fish in azure waves; fairy peach trees and borders of grapes; plum blossom and jasmine flowers; reeds and wild geese, and storks flying in clouds; and red dragons in the middle of blue sea-waves. The hidden meanings of the objects shown are sometimes interesting. Take, for instance, a flock of magpies. In China one magpie is a sign of good luck; two together symbolise a happy meeting; and a whole flock of them promise a really festive and joyful gathering.

A feature that became common in the late Ming period was the application of pipeclay or similar material to give decoration in relief. For example, vases sometimes bore designs of flowers shown in relief. In the same way bowls were made that carried as decoration projecting figures representing the Taoist Eight Immortals. The figures were in biscuit and were painted or gilded. The development of this practice of relief decoration led to some unfortunate results from the artistic point of view.

The astonishing versatility of the Chinese potters is specially evident in their command of colour. A good deal of the early stoneware was uniform in colour, although in delicate tints. A technique brought to perfection in the Ming period was the use of a brilliant white porcelain with cobalt blue underglaze decoration. Blue and white proved such an ideal colour combination that it came to occupy a position of particular regard. In the early part of the Ming dynasty a coarse kind of native cobalt was used, which gave a result that was frequently speckled with black. Later a much purer variety was imported, perhaps from Persia, and was the source of the magnificent Mohammedan blue. Even when pottery in a variety of lovely colours was at its best the simple blue and white continued to hold its own. And when finally in the late Ch'ing period the use of colours became much debased, the blue and white seemed in a much greater degree to maintain its old standard.

The Spotted Dogs of Fo and Dragon Fish-bowls

The middle of the Ch'ing period was remarkable for the production of many pieces of great size. Among these are the colossal Dogs of Fo, now in the Louvre, which are gilded and made very handsome with green and turquoise spots. Also dating from this time are huge fish-bowls, ornamented with dragons, which were installed in the Imperial Gardens for holding waterlilies and goldfish. Each of these latter bowls occupied a whole kiln while being made, and had to be fired for nineteen days.

Apple-Green and Ox-Blood Orange Decoration on Egg-shell China

The colours available under the Ch'ing dynasty were more numerous than ever before, but on the whole the use of them was less successful. Among the brilliant new colours that were introduced in this period were an apple-green and the famous *sang-de-boeuf* or ox-blood orange. Colour schemes in which green and pink predominated came to be known respectively as *famille verte* and *famille rose*. Technical advances in the making of the porcelain itself kept pace with the invention of new enamel colours, and some of the most striking coloured decoration was applied to a very fragile porcelain known to the Chinese as "bodiless," and familiar to us as egg-shell china. A magnificent colour like the *sang-de-boeuf* was very properly regarded as too good to be used in combination with others, and it was happily applied as a monochrome.

Japanese Pottery
Buddhist priests introduced the ritual drinking of tea into Japan in the 12th century. The little cups, bowls and jars used in this ceremony were originally of dark-coloured earthenware, as no porcelain was then available. Gradually the ceremony became little more than a polite social custom, but traditional forms survived, and it remained fashionable to use only primitive pottery. So the precious utensils of old dark earthenware were treasured and handed down as heirlooms in the same way as family silver is with us. And when genuine old earthenware was not available, potters imitated it and, for good measure, introduced picturesque roughness and irregularity.

The Porcelain of Japan
The collector of Oriental porcelain needs to beware of the important but sometimes not very evident distinction between the two main varieties. The Japanese does not achieve the perfection of the Chinese, being largely derivative and copied from the latter. As we have seen, there was a passionate love of fine porcelain in China at a very early date, and exquisite examples were produced. In Japan, on the other hand, the great impulse was commercial, for when the industry became organised in the middle of the 17th century it was to supply the demands of the Western world.

In spite of this it is not always simple to decide the *provenance* of particular pieces. The difficulty is that the

Japanese, always skilful copyists, imitated Chinese prototypes so well, especially those of the Ming period, that close
examination is sometimes needed to detect the difference.
There are a number of features, however, which can serve
as a guide to the collector and put him on his guard. First,
there is the quality of the material. The Chinese ware had
admirable uniformity in its texture and in its dense white
colour. The Japanese is not always quite so smooth or
even, and there may be a hint of blue or pink from impurities where no colour is intended. Then, in decoration,
there is a confidence and virility about the Chinese designs
which in the Japanese degenerates into something which is
superficially the same but which has become somewhat
effeminate.

Following early copies of Chinese ware, which continued
to be made as one line of export production, the Japanese
brought out several original types which have their own
attractions. In the 17th-century Mikôchi porcelain, while
attempting to imitate old Ming ware, managed something
novel in the way of little cups painted with boys at play
under pine trees. The cheaper cups, it was said, had just
one or two boys on them, but for a higher price, fairly
enough, more boys were added by the painter. In other
characteristic Japanese decoration great use was made of
chrysanthemums and peonies, both rather large and
clumsy flowers when used in bulk.

In Imari ware in particular the pieces are often over-
loaded with vague and indefinite patterns carried out in a
multiplicity of colours. Yet the Imari kilns for long
enjoyed great prosperity, and attracted potters from other
provinces who attempted to gain admittance by stealth so
as to learn the secrets of manufacture. When discovered
these intruders were dealt with in peculiarly horrid and
painful ways.

Gold and scarlet brocade

One of the most ,pleasing of Japanese ceramics is the porcelain of Kioto. One of the aims of the potters of this province was to copy the famous old Ming red, reputed to be "made from powdered rubies." In fact the new product had little resemblance to the old, but a good red was obtained. Little bowls were made of this red ware, and these were decorated in gold with patterns taken from textiles. The inter-relationship of crafts in this way is not uncommon, and in this case at least was highly successful. The resulting "gold and scarlet brocade" ware of Kioto attracted the attention of the West, and much of it was exported, examples of it being shown in several of our museums. Unfortunately in the generation after its introduction it became very debased.

Japanese pieces often seem clumsy in shape compared with the delicate and elusive lines of the Chinese. The decoration of Japanese ware also has a certain grossness about it, which is not found elsewhere in the East. In the early 18th century, for instance, Kaga pottery was a leading product. This frequently had the whole surface covered with enamels in sombre and sinister-looking colours, including a dark green with designs in black, purple used in conjunction with a navy-blue, and an aggressive red.

7

EUROPEAN CERAMICS

ITALY Della Robbia Pottery Plaques in a Florentine Palace—
Jugs for Drugs and other Pharmacy Pottery—*HOLLAND* Herman
of Haarlem and Tiles showing Dutch Fishing Boats—The Porcelain
of Amsterdam—*GERMANY* Dresden China—How White Powder
for Wigs came to be used for making Porcelain—German Stove
Tiles painted with Biblical Scenes—*FRANCE* Sèvres Porcelain
made for Madame de Pompadour.

Our aim in this chapter is to make a brief survey of the
history of the manufacture of pottery and porcelain on
the continent of Europe. In Italy very beautiful work was
being done in the 15th and 16th centuries by the Della
Robbia family. Dutch tiles from Delft enjoyed a high
reputation from the early 17th century. In Germany the
great Dresden China factory established its reputation in
the early part of the 18th century. From the middle of
the same century Sèvres Porcelain also became famous.
Each of these in turn made its own significant contribution
to artistic achievement and to the general body of ceramic
knowledge.

Della Robbia Plaques
The delightful Della Robbia plaques are quite distinctive,
although they have affinities with three or four other
branches of ceramic art. The founder of the dynasty was
Luca della Robbia, who was born in Florence between
1390 and 1400, and died there in 1482. He was a sculptor,
and found it helpful to do modelling in clay before cutting
stone or marble. In this way he became interested in the

71

application of white and coloured enamels to terra-cotta figures and reliefs. From the technical aspect his main achievement was to develop and improve tin enamel. Artistically, too, he used glazes with superlative skill.

The earliest work of Luca della Robbia in this medium was a bas-relief of the Resurrection made for the Cathedral of Florence. To begin with, the terra-cotta reliefs were subsidiary to marble groups; later, when their use was developed, they were given more prominence and were incorporated as an architectural feature of the interior design of buildings.

Ceramics in a Florentine Palace

The use of Della Robbia reliefs is well shown in the Guelf Palace in Florence. The great hall of the Palace was designed by Brunelleschi in 1418, and has the beauty that was characteristic of Tuscan architecture during the Renaissance. The apartment is magnificently simple and dignified, while the Madonna and Child by Luca della Robbia, which is placed over the main doorway, introduces a note of colour and richness that harmonises perfectly with the whole conception. It was decided to restore the building, now owned by the Commune, to commemorate the centenary of Dante in 1921, and the work was completed two years later.

About 1460 Lucca took into partnership his nephew Andrea (1435-1525). From this date more colours were used in the compositions, sometimes to advantage but not always with pleasing effect. The medallions of *bambini* made by Andrea are particularly lovely and appealing. The family connection was carried on in a third generation by Giovanni della Robbia (1469-1529), who shared in the triumphs of his father Andrea and his great-uncle Luca. The output of the della Robbias, remarkable for its long-sustained excellence, lasted for nearly a hundred years.

The first soft-paste porcelain in Europe was made at Florence between 1565 and 1620, produced under the patronage of the Medici family. Persian models were closely copied. In the 18th century hard-paste porcelain was made here and at Venice.

Jugs for Drugs, and other Pharmacy Pottery

Gaily painted pottery became the fashion in Italy in the 15th century. Bold, harsh colours were used, including deep shades of blue, purple, orange, green and black. The pieces were more often made for show than for use, and included plates and dishes bearing portrait medallions and paintings of figure subjects. In addition there was pottery for pharmacies, such as spouted jugs and cylindrical jars for holding drugs and syrups.

Herman of Haarlem

Pottery-making was introduced at Delft near Rotterdam, at least as early as 1584 by Herman Pietersz of Haarlem, who in 1611 was one of the Guild of St. Luke. The Guild, which afterwards became very powerful, included potters among its eight constituent corporations.

In the early 17th century one of the local Delft products consisted of tiles conceived on simple lines with a single figure of man or beast in a circle or rectangle, and a little conventional foliage or other decoration in the corner spaces. The result was lively and pleasant. As an artistic medium a border tile offers limited scope, and good taste demands restraint—here we have this restraint exercised either instinctively or consciously. Some plates of the period show similar qualities.

The manufacture of pottery at Delft was greatly expanded between the years 1651 and 1660. More elaborate work was now produced, but the less pretentious pieces, like the blue-and-white helmet jugs which retained

73

some of the characteristics of peasant craft, continued to be the most successful artistically.

Of later products here, the shapes of many vases and other pieces were much debased. Such articles as sauce-boats in the 18th century were given such complicated handles, rims and feet that the outline was tortured almost beyond belief. The painted decoration, too, was over-elaborated to such an extent that it passed out of control, offering to the eye only a confused and displeasing jumble without rhyme or reason.

Dutch Fishing Boats

Some of the Dutch blue-and-white tiles remained com-paratively good when other things had gone badly astray. Here, too, however, the later the work the worse it became. Views of herring fishing-boats, for example, while still decorative, came to be painted in rather perfunctory style. There was no longer the feeling that each was an individual work of art, but rather that an inferior and unskilled worker had been set to copy a model time after time, and was being paid by the piece. So the fishing-boats became loosely drawn and appeared hardly seaworthy, and the waves looked artificial and wooden. By such slackness are hard-earned reputations lost.

Some authorities trace strong Italian influence in the polychrome Dutch tiles made from the end of the 16th century, leading on to Chinese influence in the mono-chrome blue or purple tiles of the 18th century. While it is attractive to explore these cultural links, the essential point to observe is how national characteristics assert themselves, so that the best Dutch tiles could not possibly be mistaken for anything else.

For a long period the making of painted tiles was a speciality in Holland, and in no other form of pottery have the Dutch so excelled. To begin with their use was the usual one of a form of paving or floor-covering. Only when their artistic possibilities came to be more fully realised were they adapted for the attractive purpose of panelling fireplaces.

Amsterdam Porcelain

Hard porcelain began to be made near Amsterdam in 1764, with the help of German workers displaced by the Seven Years' War. In one form or another the factory continued until 1810, but faced constant difficulties, among them the return of the Germans to their fatherland when settled conditions were re-established, and the flooding of the country with imports of Japanese porcelain.

Dresden China

In the latter part of the 17th century a considerable amount of Chinese porcelain began to reach Europe. The princelings of the Germanic states were among those who became enthusiastic patrons of this marvellous material, and before long many attempts were being made to discover the secrets of its manufacture. The first man who proved successful in making hard porcelain in Europe was named Johann Böttcher, and his career was so romantic that it deserves special reference.

Johann was employed by William I of Prussia as an alchemist, which Rosenthal neatly describes as a position midway between a witch doctor and a chemist. His main task was to search for the philosopher's stone, an imaginary stone or mineral compound which, it was long believed, had the power of transforming base metals into gold. The Prussian ruler, like many men before him, felt that it would be a convenience to have such a means of creating wealth.

Unfortunately Böttcher was not successful in his search, and relations between him and his employer became strained. Failure might mean hanging or some equally unpleasant fate, so he decided to run away. He reached the first town in Saxony, but was there arrested upon a demand from Prussia. As it happened, however, Augustus the Strong of Saxony also needed a man who could make gold. He was an avid collector of Oriental porcelain, and was constantly needing more money for his expensive hobby. So Johann was not delivered up, being virtually kidnapped by Augustus. He was kept a prisoner and set to work first in the fortress of Königstein and later in the castle of Albrechtsburg.

Being a wise man Johann now developed a second string to his bow. Besides being forced to continue his quest for gold, he was allowed to conduct experiments with the aim of reproducing Chinese porcelain, this being fully in accordance with the wishes of his new master, and another of the enterprises in which the royal heads of Europe competed with each other.

How White Powder for Wigs came to be Used for Making Porcelain

The main obstacle which Johann faced was the usual one of not having the right materials. He tried various things, working carefully and advancing nearer and nearer to his goal. It was not, however, until a date variously stated as being between 1708 and 1711, that he was finally set upon right lines by receiving some kaolin, essential to the making of porcelain. One Schnorr had discovered a local source of the material, and was selling it as a powder for keeping wigs white.

The triumph of Johann Böttcher in making true white translucent porcelain was great good fortune for Augustus, who was not slow to exploit it. Close secrecy was observed about the composition of the porcelain, and the kaolin and other materials were brought to the fortress-factory at Meissen in sealed bags and under armed guard.

The first occasion upon which this porcelain was offered for sale to the public was at the Leipzig Fair at Easter, 1713. For some years longer Böttcher, who had been appointed Director of the factory, had to continue his researches before bulk manufacture could be established on firm lines. But when he died in 1719, at the age of 34, the experimental period was over. For generations afterwards the works continued to produce Royal Dresden China which won the admiration of the world.

Stove Tiles Painted with Biblical Scenes
Winters are cold in Germany, and slow-combustion stoves have long been popular there as an efficient and economical method of heating. At an early date, too, it was found that coating the stoves with coloured tiles made them easy to clean and much more pleasant to look at.

In the early part of the 18th century in Hamburg many white stove tiles were painted in blue. Within a fairly elaborate border were shown pictures of a number of popular types. There were Biblical scenes, such as the Judgment of Solomon, copied from Rubens; there were stories taken from Greek and Roman mythology; there were landscapes and seascapes, often incorporating views of buildings; and there were interior domestic scenes of people taking tea.

Sèvres Porcelain
In the 17th century France was still prosperous and powerful. It was therefore natural that experiments should be made there with the aim of reproducing oriental porcelain, for good ceramic ware is one of the first things desired by an aristocracy. The French were not successful in making genuine hard porcelain. In 1693 they did, however, manage to produce a new hybrid material, made partly of glass frit and partly of plastic clay, constituting

a fresh variety of soft porcelain. From this beginning sprang great developments.

Pompadour Porcelain

At Sèvres soft porcelain was made by private partners under royal patronage from the middle of the 18th century. The French king had previously aided a porcelain factory at Vincennes, and the transfer of the works to its new site took place under the influence of the notorious Madame de Pompadour, who herself lent money for the venture.

The enterprise was run on most unbusinesslike lines, and the products, which were excessively fragile, were almost unsaleable. Porcelain from Saxony was reported to be better and cheaper, while that from the Far East was still cheaper. In consequence heavy losses were incurred by the proprietors, and there was risk of complete failure.

Madame de Pompadour felt that both her pride and her pocket would be hurt if the factory was not successful, and she avoided this by persuading Louis XV to become the sole owner. This step had far-reaching consequences, for as a royal establishment Sèvres was given many privileges. In particular severe restrictions were placed upon the manufacture of porcelain elsewhere in France, especially as regards gilded or painted pieces. In addition porcelain intended for the use of the royal household, for the courtiers, or for presents to foreign ambassadors, automatically came from Sèvres. Even advantages of this kind, however, were not sufficient to prevent losses, and the making of porcelain continued to prove a serious drain on the purse of the King.

Kaolin from Limoges

So far only soft porcelain had been in question. In 1761 the secret of how to make the hard variety was brought from Germany, but it was not possible to exploit it fully because of lack of suitable material. Several more years were to elapse before supplies of good kaolin were found near Limoges. Thereafter both the soft and hard kinds were made at Sèvres until the early years of the 19th century, when the former was given up. Meanwhile, important factories for the production of hard porcelain were established at Limoges, following the natural economic law of having works on the site of raw materials.

Early Sèvres porcelain, being old and precious, tends to have a romantic aura. Looked at dispassionately, however, it is mostly in deplorably bad taste, and what followed in later years was no better. On this porcelain a lot of gilt and gaudy colours were used without discretion. There was also tasteless extravagance in ornament, first in the baroque and later in the rococo style, with an endless succession of broken curves, shells and scrolls, executed in a florid manner. Inserted in elaborate borders were paintings of flowers unlike any that ever grew in a garden, or scenes that were supposed to represent shepherds and shepherdesses in simple rustic surroundings, but in fact showed courtiers and courtesans in fancy dress with no regard for reality. The author, being conducted round the Sèvres factory on one occasion, was shown a large old vase made there many years before. The official with him described it as being "*sans prix*," but when asked if this meant "priceless," said on the contrary in this case it meant "worthless."

8

OLD ENGLISH POTTERY

The English Idiom in Pottery—Earthenware known as Delft but made at Lambeth—John Dwight's figures of Jupiter and Neptune —The Punch Bowls and Potted-fish Pots of Liverpool—Pew-groups and Cavalry-men—How the first English teapots were made— Decorating Wrotham ware—Thomas Toft, and Charles in the Oak —The white crockery of John Astbury—Wedgwood and Neo-Classicism.

The English Idiom in Pottery

The pottery made in England in the Middle Ages was very obviously a native product. It had well-marked features not related to continental wares. It was good to look at, for although homely it was bold in conception and full of character. While simple, it was well balanced and had dignity, so that taking into account the fact that nearly all of it was designed for use and not for ornament, the artistic merit was surprisingly high. It seemed the kind of pottery made for honest folk who valued sound reliable quality above mere showiness.

For a long time English pottery was not produced in quantity, being made on a small scale in many different districts. Demand in the Middle Ages was still limited, because in the 13th to 15th centuries both rich and poor still used vessels of wood and pewter for many purposes. Another limiting factor was that the spending powers of most people extended only to necessities.

In this period very few pots were made for ornament except a very limited number of special pieces to mark such occasions as births or weddings, or to demonstrate the skill

Made in London in 1632, this earthenware tankard is tin-glazed. Similar designs are often used by contemporary artists and this mug would not be out of place in the modern home. *By courtesy of the Victoria and Albert Museum.*

This exquisite porcelain shepherd and shepherdess are 9¾ inches high and hand painted in colour. They were made in Derby about 1760. *By courtesy of the Victoria and Albert Museum.*

of the craftsman. In the ordinary way they were intended for use in the cellar or the kitchen of the great houses, and for the cottage or the alehouse, designed accordingly. Actually, the pieces were often highly ornamental, but this was largely an unintentional element. It cannot be doubted that our ancestors derived aesthetic pleasure from their work as a form of self-expression, and in pleasing themselves were able to please others both of their own generation and ours.

Delft Ware

In England the name Delft was given to our equivalent of the majolica of Italy and the faience of France and elsewhere. Its manufacture here began very early in the 17th century, probably about 1600. The art of tin-enamelling was first developed by the Italians, but was copied at much the same time in England, France, Holland and Italy. Our earliest and leading place of manufacture appears to have been Lambeth.

The name suggests that we derived the art from Holland, but Church, in his *English Earthenware*, says that the style of the most characteristic pieces of delft believed by connoisseurs to have been made at Lambeth in the 17th century is distinctly Italian, not Dutch. In this he is supported by no less an expert than Dr. Glaisher, who shows that these early pieces had items of ornament and a choice of colours common to Italy but unknown in Holland. It would appear, in fact, that the manufacture was established with the help of Italians who settled in London.

There is an attractive plate of this kind of enamelled earthenware in the London Museum. It is of English workmanship and is dated 1602. The size is just over ten inches in diameter, and it is painted in blue, green, orange and yellow, besides being outlined in dark purple. In character it is something of a forerunner of the blue-dash chargers. On it is an inscription in blue letters which reads: " The rose is red, the leaves are grene, God save Elizabeth our Queene." The centre part carries a painting of a city probably intended to represent London. Another dish of this type, dated London, 1620, is 17¼ inches in diameter, and carries a composition of fruit and foliage in much the same colour scheme.

Delft ware was made only at Lambeth up to about 1675. Two other principal centres of manufacture were Bristol, from the last quarter of the 17th century, and Liverpool, which developed a little later. Blue-dash chargers were made at Bristol in the late 17th and early 18th centuries and they are among the most handsome examples of our decorative pottery.

The reason why the use of the term delft became so well established in England was probably twofold. By about 1670 Delft had gained a high reputation for this kind of ware, so that Dutch methods of making began to be copied in other countries. More important, however, was the fact that this influence became especially strong with us after the coming of William of Orange in 1688. Nevertheless, we have to keep in mind that the pioneer work was done long before this date.

A peculiarity of Lambeth delft is its slightly pink coloration. The explanation of this appears to have been that, as the local clay is unusually stiff and resistant, it will only absorb a limited amount of enamel, any excess running off. It therefore happened that the enamel was apt to be thin in places, allowing the body colour to show through.

The Stoneware of John Dwight

John Dwight of Fulham claimed to have discovered the secret of German stoneware. He took out patents in 1671 and 1684. This material was pottery fired at a sufficiently high temperature to cause it to acquire a vitrified surface that was impervious to most liquids and resistant even to acids. It was sometimes salt-glazed, but as a rule this was considered unnecessary. In colour it was usually brown, varying from a light freckled brown in Fulham to a dark lustrous brown in Nottingham. At a later date, however, the Staffordshire potters evolved an excellent white variety.

Dwight was among those who made substantial contributions to technical progress in ceramics, although not on the grand scale of Wedgwood and others. One of the ways in which he experimented was in making pottery in which a number of clays of different colours were used. By taking clays of blue, brown, grey and white he was able to obtain a variety of effects, from splashes of colour to something resembling marble. And this chromatic decoration came from the natural clays alone, without the addition of any colouring agent, and some pretty effects were obtained in this way at very low cost.

Jupiter and Neptune as Ceramic Figures

The most ambitious pieces made at the Dwight factory were ceramic statuettes. One of these is a life-sized bust of Prince Rupert, now in the British Museum, and another the pathetic half-length figure of the potter's little dead daughter Lydia, now in the Victoria and Albert Museum.

Among these pieces of fine stoneware is a statuette of Jupiter, interesting because it has a brown surface which suggests bronze. It is thought that in this and a few other cases Dwight may have copied a bronze original and kept to the same colour purposely, the effect being obtained by the use of a brown salt-glaze. This example, about a foot high, is preserved in the Liverpool City Museum. Jupiter, armed with a gilt thunderbolt, is partly draped in a flowing robe which must have been a decided help in the modelling. On the same base is rather tame-looking eagle. The date of manufacture was about 1680.

At South Kensington is a figure of Neptune which is a companion piece to the Jupiter at Liverpool and to one of Mars in the British Museum. The Neptune work, also of grey stoneware glazed to imitate bronze, shows a sturdy-looking, bearded figure. The right arm is raised, while the left hand grips a fish so tightly that it wears a very agonised expression.

At their best these statuettes are very good indeed, and there has been considerable speculation about who had the talent to model them. Some writers give the credit to Dwight himself, but as he was a plain business man this is extremely unlikely. He had, however, the gift of gathering brilliant men around him, and the most probable person is the famous Grinling Gibbons, who as a young man was for a time in his employ.

The Golden Lion of the Whale Fishery

In the course of the 18th century Liverpool became a ceramic centre of some note. Among the articles commonly produced here were delft punch-bowls, often painted in blue with an accurate drawing of one or other of the ships that sailed from the port. The pieces often bore inscriptions which now form interesting records of the period. One such note read: " Made for Captain Metcalfe, who commanded *the Golden Lion*, the first vessel that sailed out of Liverpool on the whale fishing and Greenland trade, and presented to him on his return from his second voyage by his employers, a company composed of the principal merchants of Liverpool, in the year 1753."

One of the most active of the Liverpool potters was Zachariah Barnes (1743-1820). At his works in the old Haymarket he made such things as druggists' jars, potted-fish pots and round dishes of extra large size. These last were sent to Wales, where it was the custom in many households to feed from a common dish, into which all the members dipped their spoons. But as a port Liverpool sent some of its products much further afield than Wales, a good deal of the local delft, for example, being sent overseas to the then English colonies in America.

Pew Groups in Salt-Glazed Ware

Among the most amusing and extraordinary things ever made in pottery are the groups, usually of two figures, shown sitting on a bench or pew. Although crude and naïve these pieces of salt-glazed ware have a certain endearing quality about them. Pairs of lovers sit holding hands, or Adam and Eve stand solemnly by a tree, the result being surprisingly fresh and quaint. Incidentally, if the story of the Fall were not so well known, it would sometimes appear from these groups that Eve was feeding an eager and half-starved serpent with the apple and not the other way round. There is such complete absence of sophistication that the pieces might well belong to the Middle Ages rather than to the first half of the 18th century.

Lead Glazed Cavalrymen

The lead-glazed figures of the second half of the 18th century were often quite as quaint as their predecessors. We have companion pieces of cavalrymen in elaborate uniforms mounted on disproportionately tiny horses with curly tails; plump cats or rabbits with smug expressions; or, as in the case of a specimen in the Willett Collection at the Brighton Museum, a man on horseback with a woman riding pillion behind him. The horse is the most wooden piece imaginable, yet at the same time is a nice cheerful-looking beast, while the two figures are shown in their Sunday-best, the woman in a stylish hat and a very tight-waisted dress.

It is not easy to analyse the vitality which these figures

undoubtedly possess. The body may have a head which is just a round knob, and the legs and arms may be represented by miserable straight thin pipes of clay. The features may be indicated merely by a conventional shorthand system of dots and dashes. But in spite of these handicaps the pieces capture the imagination and are full of life and movement, so that the affectionate regard in which they have always been held is readily understandable.

By about 1800 groups were being made, at Leeds and elsewhere, which were a good deal more naturalistic. While pleasant enough in their way these had not so much character as earlier ones, and therefore not the same appeal. From then onwards more was attempted, as, for example, in an early 19th century figure of a sailor in the Brighton Museum, but a certain *joie de vivre* seems to have been lost, and instead we have something made merely to meet a demand. From this time the modellers are evidently no longer unsophisticated.

How English Teapots Were First Made

Until late Stuart times, or towards the end of the 17th century, the national drinks were ale, cider and mead although wealthy people also drank imported wines. When the drinking of tea and coffee was introduced, the silver goblets and drinking glasses from which the fashionable world had taken its wine were no longer suitable, for the new beverages were served hot, and accordingly substitute containers had to be found.

To begin with, the East India merchants imported with the tea itself some Chinese teapots and cups in red stoneware. Although the material from which these were made was of good quality, their price was high because of the great distance they had to travel, the more so as heavy breakage took place on the way. There was a lucrative market open, therefore, for potters in Europe who could imitate them and the Dutch, among others, were successful in producing this kind of ware in what became known as "red porcelain."

The pioneers of this line in England were two brothers, David and John Elers, who appear to have come over with William of Orange. David is said to have had some training in ceramics but John was a silversmith; both, however, found work with Dwight at Fulham, and became interested in research under his inspiring leadership. They succeeded in producing an excellent red stoneware and established their own pottery to exploit it. Their aim from the beginning was to make tea services, and they were fortunate in placing their product on the market just when tea-drinking was becoming more general, so that their business enjoyed considerable prosperity.

Slipware

Slip is formed by diluting clay until it takes the form of a creamy syrup. In this state it can be trailed on the surface of pottery to give decorative patterns. This must have been a very early method of ornamentation, and in the British Museum some fragments of slipware are preserved that were found at Kirkstall and Fountains Abbey. This so-called Cistercian ware was a hard red pottery with a lustrous brown-black glaze, decorated with white slip. At the Reformation this activity appears to have died out, not to be renewed for a century or two, and then resumed in a different form.

In the late 17th and early 18th centuries a kind of English slipware was developed which, while conforming to national standards of restraint and good taste, was of such excellence that it has retained the esteem of connoisseurs. The pieces that survive have good shapes, a rich lead glaze and very pleasant soft colouring, usually shades of brown and yellow that harmonise well. The designs formed by the slip are very quaint and lively, incorporating many figure subjects, such as royal personages, lions and unicorns, pelicans and mermaids. Some of these creations while almost grotesque remain attractive. Incorporated in the designs we sometimes find the names of the owners or the potters, together with dates.

Wrotham Ware and its Decoration

The revival of English slipware appears to have begun at Wrotham in Kent very early in the 17th century, and here its manufacture was continued for well over a hundred years. Later, as we shall see, there was the activity of Thomas Toft in Staffordshire, followed by the development of other centres at Bolsover, Cockpit Hill and Tickenhall in Derbyshire.

Wrotham ware is very distinctive. Instead of the flat plates which were popular elsewhere, the factory concentrated on posset pots and tygs. In addition all the candlesticks of the period that were decorated with slip appear to have been made there. The most remarkable feature of this ware, however, is its decoration, which incorporated more extensive use of slip than anything that had been seen before. Wrotham is in fact celebrated for the elaborate and ornate slipware which it produced.

Slip was used on the Wrotham pottery in both the trailed and pressed forms. When the ornament was "applied" the stamped devices, on circular or rectangular bases, carried coats-of-arms, dates, initials and rosettes among other things. These little pressings were multiplied manyfold and were the main features of the decoration, the trailed slip serving the subordinate purpose of framing them or linking them together. They look very English, but the technique may have been continental in origin. It is perhaps significant that Kent was readily accessible to foreign influence, and that later developments in

Staffordshire were on quite different and more native lines.

The earliest piece ascribed to Wrotham is in the Liverpool City Museum and is dated 1612. It is a cylindrical tyg of red clay with a yellowish lead glaze, and has four double-looped handles. There is stamped ornament in relief, showing fleur-de-lys, sunflowers and rosettes in white touched with green. Another surviving piece is an elaborately decorated candlestick of 1649, preserved in the Victoria and Albert Museum.

The latest known specimen of Wrotham pottery is a small two-handled cup of red clay with white slip decoration. It is dated 1721, and is three inches high by about five inches in diameter including the handles.

Of the Wrotham potters, two whose names are known to us were Nicholas Hubble and George Richardson. There is some evidence to suggest that for a number of years after production had ceased at the place itself, potters who had been trained there continued to work at the neighbouring village of Kemsing.

Thomas Toft and Charles in the Oak

The greatest name in connection with English slipware is that of Thomas Toft. Where he was born is not known, but we can claim with confidence that he was a Staffordshire man, for all the surviving specimens of his work have been found in the county, and all his followers worked there. Many good judges consider that, from the artistic point of view, the very finest examples of slipware are those made by him.

Thomas Toft was producing from about 1670, and his brother or son, named Ralph, from a few years later. They seem to have confined themselves almost entirely to dishes, but there is a cup bearing the name of Thomas Toft in the museum at York. The decoration of Toft ware is on the lines already indicated. There are heads of kings reduced to bare essentials with no attempt to capture a likeness, but which are nevertheless extremely lively studies. The real and imaginary creatures shown are also vividly drawn in a crude and unsophisticated way, some of them comical and some coy, but all full of vigour.

But not all of even the Toft pieces were decorated in this way, some of them being simpler in conception. For example, one deep dish made by Thomas Toft about 1670 had as the main feature of its decoration a fleur-de-lys in the centre. Apart from this, and a cartouche bearing the maker's name, there is just a pattern of overlapping discs and a trellis border.

One of the most famous of the Toft dishes shows King Charles in the Oak. The head of Charles is shown peeping through foliage with the royal supporters on either side. This dish, which is a little over 20 inches in diameter, is of reddish buff ware with a wash of white clay inside, and the slip decoration is in brown, red and white.

Another sportive example is an Adam and Eve dish. In the centre is the tree shown in white and green. Although the tree appears to be only in the flowering stage, the serpent wound round its trunk has secured an apple from somewhere, which it is duly presenting to a figure on the left labelled EVE, while the design is balanced by another figure on the right labelled ADAM. This important piece, about 22 inches in diameter, has other charming decorative features, including a flying angel and a cockatrice; a rabbit and a bird; and a border of tulips. It is inscribed THOMAS TOFT in green letters, this colouring being exceedingly rare.

The Toft tradition survived for a time, as is shown in a saucer-shaped dish with a narrow slanting rim and notched edge made about 1700. It is rather smaller than those already mentioned, being $16\frac{3}{4}$ inches in diameter. The design consists simply of an owl surrounded by owlets and beyond them an open cable border. Owls can be curious looking at any time, but these are more so than most.

These dishes have great individuality, and, as all the slip was applied freehand, each of them is in fact unique. In this they are unlike most continental pieces, where the slip was often moulded and then stuck on. Unfortunately even in England true slip decoration had only a short run, for by about 1750 the moulded type had become prevalent here also.

The dish form was chosen for these pieces decorated with trailed or moulded slip because this gave the maximum space for display; it was, in fact, intended as something that could be hung on a wall for ornament. Some of them suffered indignity later in their careers, for they have been dug up in farmyards, showing signs of wear as if used to feed the chickens. But this treatment took place only long after their original proud owners had been gathered to their fathers.

John Astbury and White Crockery

The Astbury family was of some consequence in the history of pottery. John (1688-1743), was trained in the establishment of the Elers brothers at Bradwell in Staffordshire, and afterwards set up his own pottery at Shelton. His brother Samuel, also a potter, married Elizabeth Wedgwood, aunt of the celebrated Josiah. Although he died comparatively young, John Astbury made a fortune; his connection with the pottery industry was continued by his son Thomas who is credited with introducing cream-coloured ware.

There were constant efforts on the part of the potters to make their earthenware resemble porcelain both in its intrinsic quality and in its whiteness. Early in the 18th century Thomas Astbury obtained good results by using a wash of white pipeclay, brought from Bideford in Devon, over coloured local clays. The method was, of course, very

91

like that of tin-enamelling delft ware, which provided a white coating in the same way.

Some years later, about 1720, a further advance took place, which was to use calcined flints in the mixture so that the body became white throughout. Both Astbury and Thomas Heath of Lane Delph have claims to the credit of this invention. This fine material could be made thin, and with its whiteness and translucency would have been something of a rival to porcelain if it had not had a rough surface resembling wash-leather or orange-peel.

The search for perfection never ends and it was inevitable that the potters should set themselves some new problem to solve. The next quest undertaken in this case was to provide the white crockery with a smooth surface. This was done successfully by adding lead to the glaze, which increased the thickness of the ware and therefore lessened the resemblance to porcelain.

In considering these achievements of the past, there is some risk of feeling that we have come to a standstill in our own day and generation, for we can neither foretell the future nor see completely the changes actually in progress. We can be certain, however, that just as Old English Pottery evolved, so we ourselves are making history. And with modern technology and organised research there is no doubt that it is with mounting acceleration that we are moving forward towards a better world, so that there is every reason to believe that our descendants will enjoy pottery of yet undreamt of loveliness.

Wedgwood and Neo-Classicism

The career of Josiah Wedgwood (1730-95), is of absorbing interest because his boundless mental energy, combined with great strength of character and an enterprising disposition, enabled him to develop very fruitful activities in several directions at once. One major undertaking was his study of antique pottery and his successful reproduction of it. This had been done rather badly by others, dealing with a very few pieces at high cost; Wedgwood set himself a very high standard of quality, produced in bulk, and made a fortune.

In the 18th century much attention was paid to the classical tradition, and this interest was stimulated by discoveries at Herculaneum and elsewhere. The finds as usual included many pieces of pottery, and in 1767 Wedgwood became acquainted with the fine illustrations of these ceramics appearing in the *Recueil d'Antiquités Egyptiennes, Etrusques, Grecques, Romaines et Gauloises* of the Comte de Caylus. He saw the possibilities, looked up similar books and began manufacture of this line.

There are a number of points to be noticed here. The first is that Wedgwood was a pioneer in this enterprise. Before this no one had thought of applying neo-classicism to pottery on a commercial scale, and for a period he continued to have the field to himself so far as fine stoneware was concerned. His example was copied by the English porcelain factories after 1770 and at later dates by those of France and Germany, but it was he who had given the lead.

The second point is that Wedgwood made no mistake about what would suit the public. He set a fashion and created a great demand for vases and other pieces in classical form. Granted these circumstances, his business ability and technical knowledge enabled him to organise production, and then to expand still further by increasing his range of products in this style. He became especially famous for vases with relief decoration in white on bodies of pale blue, green or lilac-coloured Jasper. In due course he had a large staff engaged in making these vases and this was the first time pottery intended solely for ornament had been produced in bulk. No doubt the time was ripe, but the opportunity might have been neglected by a lesser man.

In his "useful" pottery Wedgwood also exploited some ideas which seem remarkably up-to-date and progressive, including standardisation and division of labour. In his day something of a revolution was taking place in the kind of pottery that people used in their homes. Closer attention to hygiene created a demand for ware that was non-porous and easily cleaned. In accomplishing what was required in this direction there came about a further change, namely, the production of white ware in place of the earlier red and brown types. We have seen that Wedgwood's uncle, John Astbury, took a leading part in this enterprise.

The change from a variety of cheerful warm colours to the cold uniformity of white was not altogether attractive to the eye, whatever the advantages which the new crockery might bring to the health. Wedgwood counteracted this by paying special attention to shape. He employed the best designers he could get, in order that his tableware should be elegant and pleasing, and at the same time suited to its purpose and adapted to large-scale production.

9

PRACTICE IN POTTING

How potting lends itself to handicraft teaching in schools, and how this gives children an insight into which pottery shapes are good and what decoration is appropriate—The advanced courses and professional training given in colleges of art—Creative expression and artistic maturity—Refresher courses for pottery teachers—Art training in the factory—Studio potters: their difficulties and triumphs.

Potting at School

One of the main problems in education is to make the best possible use of the infinite variety of talent and capacity which schoolchildren possess. A select few show themselves capable not only of entering grammar schools but of taking a full academic course leading to a university education. Others have ability of a different kind, which may well take a practical form.

It has been found that potting is a very popular course when facilities are provided for it in the senior classes of grammar, modern and technical schools. It has proved suitable for boys and girls between the ages of fifteen and eighteen. Once a school pottery has been set up one of the most absorbing pursuits is that of making slipware. Slip is, of course, potter's clay in a semi-liquid state, and to-day the term slipware must include pottery cast from slip in bulk. What we are concerned with here, however, is the older use applied to pottery formed by hand but decorated with slip.

It is great fun for young people to make pots while they

are still at school. The materials have to be prepared, there is need to learn how to co-ordinate hand and eye in the shaping, attention needs to be given to the details of firing and so on. Thus there is clearly a strong appeal to the practical student, who is provided with both manual work and training in organisation. What may be considered more important, however, is the opportunity that occurs of acquiring some knowledge of aesthetic considerations. To learn how to turn a pot gives an insight into what constitutes a good shape. The application of decoration, although vastly aided by a natural artistic gift, does give experience of what is appropriate.

More Advanced Courses

Pottery-making is a favourite subject of instruction in regional colleges of art and similar establishments. It is natural for students, whether young or adult, to wish to acquire some kind of manual skill. There is not a great deal of opportunity to do this in the modern world, although it is one of the reasons people learn to play the piano, ride a cycle or drive a car. It is an instinct to learn how to co-ordinate the senses of sight and touch, and to exercise it gives lasting pleasure.

Drawing and painting form an essential background for art students. When we turn to handicrafts the choice open to art schools is wide, but there are good reasons why pottery-making is one of the most popular. Working in metal is a slow business, and, at least where silver is concerned, the material is expensive. Carving in wood or stone makes very severe demands upon its devotees. Rugmaking, weaving and embroidery are useful arts but comparatively unexciting. In fact, for the majority of these students, nothing gives such enjoyment and satisfaction as clay modelling and the production of pottery.

Creative Expression

The joy of creative expression is constantly found in the making of pottery by hand. To shape a pot at all requires a degree of skill that does not come easily, but demands a good deal of concentration and patience in the learning. And once the foundations have been laid there are infinite possibilities ahead, both in making shapes that are technically difficult and in finding those which satisfy the eye because of their grace and beauty.

The advanced practitioner is not content with shaping on the wheel, for the decoration of pottery opens up another world of delight, in which the artistic sense can be applied to design and colour. Here again the only limit lies in what the student is capable of achieving. Exhibitions of students' work show not only a remarkably high standard of quality, but such variety of conception as to reveal clearly how fully their individuality has been expressed.

Artistic Maturity

One surprising thing in such work is how artistically mature is the decoration conceived by the younger students, for apparently ability in this direction is a gift that can be cultivated but not implanted. A characteristic of the designs evolved by students and other amateurs is that at their best they have a freshness lacking in the kind of commercial work, now happily becoming rarer, which depends too much on the debased copying of old patterns.

Of those who attend pottery courses at art schools and colleges, some wish to take up the work professionally, while others regard it as a recreation. It is the kind of occupation chosen because of a real sense of vocation, rather than for other reasons. When students have completed their courses they may enter one of the main branches of the pottery industry, or may become studio potters, or may themselves become instructors to following generations at art colleges. Those who take up potting for fun are so numerous that the attraction of the hobby is evidently strong, especially when we consider that few have the means of practising it at home.

Specialisation

For those students who intend to earn their livelihood by pottery it is necessary to carry studies to an advanced level. This involves specialisation, which allows scope for individual preferences. Those whose power lies in draughtsmanship may draw the shapes of pots that are to be made afterwards by others. Those who like the feel of clay and and find in it a creative medium may take up the modelling of figures. Decoration of pottery offers wide scope, and attracts many who are content to come in at this late stage of the work.

We are all subject to the artistic influences of our day and generation. This applies even to the great masters, although in their case their work may have its effect on numerous followers, so that the effect is reciprocal. It is therefore inevitable that there should be a certain family resemblance between the pottery made at the different art schools at a particular time. For this reason it is specially important that instructors should not impose their own ideas too rigidly on promising students, but should allow them to give full play to their imaginations, for originality is a precious thing that should be encouraged.

Refresher Courses

For several years past a Summer School in Pottery has been held at the Stoke-on-Trent College of Art. The course is arranged by the Ministry of Education in co-operation with the Principal of the College, and is intended for teachers.

Refresher courses of this nature have great value for those taking part, and a few dozen teachers are attracted to each course from all parts of the country. They come not only from colleges of art, but from grammar schools, teachers' training colleges and so on.

Apart from a pleasant communal life, such courses can be of absorbing interest. For success and full enjoyment, combined with professional benefit, there has to be a judicious blending of lectures, demonstrations, and works visits. At Stoke this has been achieved remarkably well, and the course has had the advantage of instruction from the College Principal, heads of Pottery Departments at other leading Schools of Art, art directors and principal designers from famous pottery firms and art experts from the Royal College of Art in London.

As all those attending are trained men and women, holding responsible teaching positions themselves, it is appropriate that there is a friendly and informal atmosphere at courses of this kind. The intention is to widen knowledge by experimenting with unfamiliar techniques, and to solve problems by discussion with others of equal status. Incidentally, quite a lot of hard work is involved, the more so as the courses are kept thoroughly practical.

Outline of Course

The method of procedure is usually along the following lines: First a lecturer gives an outline of the theoretical side of a particular problem. Then in the course of a works visit an opportunity is provided for watching a demonstration giving practical solutions. Upon returning to College the students try their hand at reproducing what they have learnt and seen, and although experts in their own lines, they may be doing something that is quite new to them. Finally, there is appraisal and criticism from the instructors and from their fellows.

A fruitful field for experiment is in connection with decoration. If you have never had the chance of painting pottery in the Picasso manner you are now able to do so, and it is surprising what influence this artist has had. What is more exciting than to draw inspiration from such a master and then evolve designs that are distinctively your own! The shape of the pot, the pattern you put on it, and the colour-scheme are probably all experimental so far as you are concerned. Then, like the student at a cookery class, the responsibility is yours of seeing your pieces through the firing and other finishing operations. With such a programme there is no danger of getting bored.

Art Training in the Factory

A number of pottery firms have facilities for training on the artistic side within their own establishments. The need for this arises in several ways and often the reason is closely linked with welfare, because it is one way of looking after new members of the staff, most of whom are young, by arranging for them to do work for which they have aptitude, and by enabling them to qualify for advancement.

Some potteries are famous for particular types of ware, and even if new entrants have had basic training elsewhere they have to learn how to apply the decoration and so on for which their employers have a market. Firms not only have their own methods for standard products, but there is also the case of specialities. If a company has artistic products for which it has established a reputation, it may well wish to keep some of the methods of manufacture confidential. For the making of pottery that comes in this category there are obvious advantages in having training at the works rather than at an art school.

The Studio Potters

In Devon and Cornwall, and in other places where good

clay is available, fairly numerous hand-potteries are still at work. These are generally run by people with artistic leanings and some art training, who have succumbed to the fascination of turning pottery. The scale of operation is very flexible, so that a livelihood can be provided for a single person, a married couple or a small community. When a group of people of kindred tastes are associated in an enterprise of this kind a very happy atmosphere can be created and maintained.

Private enterprise often makes exceedingly heavy demands on those who practise it, and yields the maximum of satisfaction with the minimum of financial reward. Studio potting in particular calls for very special qualities in its devotees. Apart from the operational side there is, for example, the financial aspect. Considerable courage must be needed to launch the venture and risk personal savings. The initial outlay on equipment is substantial in itself, but is probably less than the working capital that is also required.

At least a few years can be expected to pass before the studio potter finds his feet properly, and in the meantime his business may be more of a liability than an asset. If, as is often the case, his interest or impulse is mainly artistic to begin with, he will no doubt have acquired some practical training and experience. Nevertheless, when a man is working on his own responsibility for the first time, and is using new equipment, teething troubles are inevitable.

Selling the Goods

The strictly commercial aspects of the enterprise frequently cause anxiety for a while. Has the potter's studio been placed in a good position for attracting visitors, or has he a flair for publicity which will enable him to sell his wares at a distance? Can he gauge the local demand and make the kind of pottery wanted, or can he produce something in such a distinctive style that it creates its own demand? Survival in business may depend upon the successful answering of questions such as these, and the solutions are seldom found quickly or easily.

Fortunately there is a steady demand for hand-made artistic pottery in the more fashionable resorts and in historic towns that are visited by cultured people. Pottery of this kind is convenient and attractive as souvenirs or as presents for friends. The cost is moderate and there is a wide range of sizes available in pottery that is of a useful nature or purely ornamental. If the studio potter can evolve a style that is pleasing to the eye, say by having bright colours that fit in with a holiday mood, he should not lack custom. At the same time there is always the probability of competition from the mass-produced article.

The painting of pottery by hand may be all very well when the artist has sufficient original talent to contribute something definite from his own personality. This is often the case in a modest way with studio potters. But the proportion of these gifted folk is small, and their output is very limited. It is in the nature of the case that we have to choose between the rare offering of the artist in its original form and something that is reproduced many times.

Porridge in Peebles and Clotted Cream in Clovelly

Purchasers are attracted by pottery that has a marked character or flavour of its own. A district in Hampshire, in the West Country, or in Scotland may have certain traditional styles of pottery as regards use, shape, decoration and so on. If there is a demand for porringers in Peebles and dishes for clotted cream in Clovelly, it is wise to do something to meet it. In Britain there are almost countless examples of this kind of thing, and when visitors buy pottery with tradition behind it they feel, quite rightly, that they are getting something that really has local associations, and is therefore likely to remind them of what they have seen and done.

Another way in which a distinctive style arises is when a foreign element is introduced. From time to time partnerships are arranged between Italian, Spanish, Polish and other settlers in Britain, and descendants of our own potting families. Pots produced under these conditions frequently have an indefinably exotic look. The shape of spout or handle may be outside normal experience in this country. The colour scheme may be unexpected, or some other feature may be unusual. Whatever it is gives welcome variety, for life would be very dull if everything were strictly uniform.

10

POTTERY OF TODAY

Doodling designs in contemporary pottery decoration—The appeal of the abstract, and the contrast between Eastern and Western idioms—Some features of originality in design—The willow pattern —Stylised sprays and other good present-day ornamentation— Bowls and vases for displaying flowers—The footprints of Man Friday—Adaptation of the traditional, and the " New Look " in pottery—Squaring the circle in modern tableware and some preposterous pottery.

Doodling Designs

A good deal of contemporary ornamentation of pottery looks like inspired doodling—probably because in essence that is just what it is. Ceramic decoration is undergoing a powerful impulse which is to be found also in all the graphic arts, and notably in textile designing. The movement may be described as a flight from conventional representation into more abstract fields. What has already been accomplished includes some of the most characteristic work of our time.

Nature presents us with a host of ready-made patterns that are highly decorative. The aim, however, has been to go beyond this, and to search for a basis of pure design. This may appear to be unduly ambitious, or to be attempting the impossible, but in practise some excellent results have been achieved, together with a proportion of failures. A great deal of pleasure too, can be obtained from exercising one's ingenuity in working out abstract designs.

The limitations of natural designs can readily be appreciated. The daisy is a charming flower, and is appropriate decoration for small side-plates, but when the scale is altered and we are dealing with a large dinner-plate there it loses its nice suitability. The flower may look well, too, on a round dish but not on an oval one. In colour even we are denied a free hand, because any deliberate falsification of a natural object is not in accordance with our sense of fitness.

The Appeal of the Abstract

By contrast let us consider those single or interlaced whorls which have been used so effectively for decorating pottery. The design is not only abstract but fluid and the addition of a few more ribbon-like scrolls, or a slight rearrangement of the existing ones, will give a perfect adaptation of a circular lay-out to an oval one, so that suites can have their decoration matching in a way that is graceful and without rigidity. Interesting effects can be obtained by introducing differences in the width of the scrolls, and by contrasting narrow and wide ones in the same pattern. Colours can be varied at will according to individual choice and what appears to be the most harmonious combination, and they can be made deep or light in shade.

There is a good deal of art in all this. When elegant curving lines are woven together to form a subtle and intricate pattern the result may look more casual than is really the case. Yet the doodling element remains, perhaps more truly than in the apparently quite haphazard patterns found in some pottery where it seems that the designer, armed with a brush and a pot of paint, has been playing a slap-dash game of noughts and crosses, or merely scattering splashes.

These and other modern examples have in common at least a determination not to be bound by inherited ideas or any other sort of pre-conceived notion. An exercise which a famous art teacher gives his students at an early stage in their course is to ask them to rid their minds of thoughts of any particular external object, and then to draw at random. It is not an easy thing to do, but he considers that some of the best and most original design-embryos he has ever known germinated in this way.

The Contrasting Decoration of the East and the West

The attention paid to abstract design in decoration is a major development in our generation, and there is almost unlimited scope for further research along these lines. In the past one of the main distinguishing marks between East and West has depended upon just this feature. In Persia, for example, the most beautiful and elaborate geometrical patterns have been evolved for pottery, mosaics, carpets and textiles, while in Europe the emphasis has been on figure subjects and representations of fruit and flowers.

The intricacy of the design in Oriental work is often so great that the eye is incapable of grasping all the detail at once. This is restful to the mind, because the pattern becomes unobtrusive while still serving its purpose. If, in the European manner, a spider is depicted on a plate, the attention is constantly attracted to it, not from inclination but from necessity, so that it comes to have a nuisance value. An Oriental pattern, on the other hand, is like background music, soothing at all times but making little demand upon us unless we are in the mood to study it carefully.

Originality in Design

It is extremely difficult to strike a really original note in design, though it is comparatively easy to think out variants of an old theme. These may be quite good, and may have a certain degree of freshness about them, but only within limits that do not make any very serious demands upon the imagination. There have been a great many versions of the famous willow pattern, but, however debased the copies may be, the source of inspiration is immediately evident.

There is often a tendency to attempt to play safe by keeping to a well-established pattern in spite of gradually falling sales. This comes about because it is frequently impossible to tell in advance what the reaction of the public will be to any individual new design. You may have a potential best-seller, or something that is fated to be a complete flop.

If the art direction of a firm is in the hands of people with a good sense of design it is rewarding to go forward confidently with the marketing of something fresh at fairly short intervals. If courage is shown in this respect, and the designs chosen are of a reasonable standard, the majority of them should sell decidedly better than something that is *vieux jeu*.

Stylised Sprays

One very charming and effective form of contemporary decoration is that in which the centre of the plate is occupied by a simple stylised spray of leaves and flowers. As well as being reduced to conventional form, the flowers are often shown in little more than outline, with the minimum of shading. A small plate may carry a pair of flower-heads, and a larger one may have three. Designs of real elegance in this style have been evolved by Truda Carter, A.R.C.A., for the Poole Potteries.

Pottery of this kind represents the mood of today very accurately. It is gay and unpretentious, so that it lends itself admirably to informal entertaining. It is like a breath of fresh air after the over elaborate and pompous stodginess of so much pottery of the last century. There has been a marked change in our social habits, with casual supper parties in place of large stiff dinner parties, and this is properly represented by corresponding changes in the character of the pottery used. It is interesting that with our more modest aims we have achieved much more good pottery than our grandparents had.

Pottery for Floral Displays

Some of the most lovely contemporary pottery takes the form of bowls or vases for holding flowers. Everyone likes to have flowers about the house, so that there is a large and steady demand for receptacles for them. Today with the charges of florists so high, pots for this purpose are often designed with a narrow neck to take just two or three choice blooms or perhaps a spray of hazel, willow or larch catkins.

As the purpose of a flower-vase is to display flowers, the vase itself should be unobtrusive. Sometimes in the past this basic principle has not been borne in mind, and in consequence flower-pottery has been made in queer shapes and decorated with a patchwork of startling colours, so that the delicate tints of the flowers themselves are killed.

The question is largely one of function. If a piece of pottery is intended to serve as an ornament itself, it forms a unity and the designer is not subject to any restrictions. There is an interesting distinction here between bowls and vases. The bulb bowls in which we grow spring flowers indoors are intended just for this purpose, and are best when of a blue-green or similar colour without any decoration. Being low they are naturally inconspicuous compared with the relatively tall daffodils, tulips or hyacinths. Vases, on the other hand, by standing higher are more easily seen, and present much more surface that can be decorated. In consequence they are much more frequently chosen to serve as works of art in their own right, and are sometimes pressed into service as flower-holders only when nothing else is handy.

The Footprints of Man Friday

Not long ago a notable success in contemporary design was achieved in Wedgwood's " Man Friday " pattern. This was strikingly original and showed real imagination. It consisted simply of a double line of black footprints, very cleverly drawn, meandering across the plate in an aimless, natural sort of way, with a few palm fronds beside them. The effect was highly decorative.

An excellent piece of lighthearted decoration such as this is more likely to be the outcome of the exuberance of youth than of the conventional outlook of age, and is a plea for letting young designers have their head. Such a *tour de force* warrants designers thinking things out afresh, and not allowing themselves to become too hidebound by the textbook and academic tradition. An ounce of spontaneity is worth a ton of material that has been re-hashed, but only the best type of brain is capable of producing it.

Adaptation of the Traditional

There is, of course, no need to abandon the traditional entirely, for by natural evolution and modification it can become as much a part of the contemporary scene as anything else. When the new translucent china of Royal Doulton was introduced in 1961, one of the designs for it, "Old Colony," although essentially up-to-date, was in the 18th century tradition. Another pattern which this firm brought out at the same time was known as the "Burgundy." Although based on grapes and vine leaves, than which nothing is more conventional, it was so original in its layout and in its subtle colouring, that it quickly won the regard of an appreciative public.

The " New-Look " in Pottery

Several makes of contemporary pottery are very good indeed as regards one or more of the elements of good design determined by shape, colour and decoration. In many ways these are quite distinctive, and worthily representative of today.

Shapes are often simple and sensible. But the apparent simplicity of line is deceptive, for upon close examination we find that one of the reasons why we like a particular set of pottery is that it has subtle curves that appeal to the eye. The basic shapes may be straightforward and practical, but the proportions are good, and we get right away from the commonplace by unobtrusive turning of lip, flange or base. By comparison pottery of exaggerated shape, with parts sliced away and so on, looks not only vulgar but silly in an unsophisticated way. It is rather a curious fact that pottery in good taste often unintentionally gives the impression of having an agreeable element of sophistication, while pottery in bad taste suggests the opposite.

Good shape can be based on various principles. The aim might be to prevent chipping, which eventually leads to breakage and loss of the article. To have all edges, flanges, knobs and spout-lips well-rounded helps greatly towards this desirable end, and the resultant flowing lines can certainly be very attractive, as instanced, for example, in the admirable design of the Denby casseroles of Joseph Bourne & Son Ltd.

Squaring the Circle

Our age has been characterised by a good deal of highly original and very fresh and spontaneous work in the decoration of pottery. The considerations that apply to share are rather different, for a host of patterns can go on to a few basic shapes. In decoration human ingenuity has almost limitless scope, but form is largely indicated by nature. There is real risk, therefore, that if we interfere with natural shapes the result may vary from the slightly eccentric to the absolutely monstrous.

One of the most recent developments is to experiment with the shapes of tableware. Through the centuries plates and saucers have always been round, and cups circular in section; now in many cases they are no longer so. The outcome is charming because it has been done with perceptive delicacy. If a compromise between a circle and a square has been chosen, there has been enough discretion to ensure that the new shape is a good one.

Simply to turn a circle into a square would be crude, but to make a plate which gives the impression of being square with rounded corners has infinite possibilities, because the rounding can be varied to any degree. This gives the designer the opportunity of gauging just what most pleases the eye, and in this some of the tea and dinner services now being introduced succeed admirably. A slight modification of the familiar gives a welcome change without exaggeration or striving after effect. Among others H. Aynsley & Co. Ltd. have done some pleasant work of this kind.

What may be termed naturalistic shapes are another departure that is finding favour. These include side-plates shaped like lettuce leaves, for serving salad with hot dishes in the American manner, and fish-shaped dishes for serving *hors d'oeuvres*.

Preposterous Pottery

Not all contemporary work is good: quite a lot of ornamental pottery of preposterous shapes is sold. At first sight it seems almost incredible that a market can be found for such products, especially as bad shapes are often accompanied by crude and garish decoration. It is, however, reassuring to notice that most of this kind of pottery goes to the cheaper shops, and is evidently purchased only by an uncritical section of the public. Some of it rises very little above that of the "china" that used to be offered as prizes on fairgrounds.

There is a reassuring balance here, for several of the leading manufacturers have impeccable taste in such matters, and evidently cater for customers who have equally high standards. In the past the extremes of fashion have often been the least acceptable to cultivated taste. It is accordingly most encouraging to observe how much really charming pottery is available today in the best shops and stores. Surely there are more pots of good shape and pleasant decoration now offered for sale than was ever the case in the past.

An early morning teaset which comprises five pieces. White on blue jasper, thrown and engine turned, it was made in 1784. The reliefs are by Lady Templeton of "Domestic Employment" and on the teapot which is 4 inches high, by "Poor Maria." *By courtesy of Josiah Wedgwood and Sons Limited.*

This coffee set is an example of Poole pottery and is made in various two-tone finishes; here it is red and white. Note the simple but pleasing shapes of the cups and pots. *By courtesy of Carter, Stabler and Adams Ltd.*

11

THE GENTLE ART OF COLLECTING

The difference between true collecting and the accumulation of oddments—The qualities needed in a collector and the fields open to his enterprise—The advantages of paying attention to quality and of breaking new ground—Fakes and forgeries—The pleasures of visiting old towns and the advantages of keeping records of purchases made on such occasions—How fashion can take unfortunate directions, as in the case of Rockingham ware—The Lowestoft tradition—The care of curios as regards methods of cleaning—The display cabinet—Collecting as a social amenity.

Parrot's Eggs and Petrified Peaches

The collecting instinct is strong in most of us, but to be effective needs to be given direction. Boswell Lancaster mentions that when Sir Hans Sloane's antiquities were acquired for the nation they were found to include such items as "a petrified peach, a cinder from the burning Vesuvius, a parrot's egg laid at Chelsea and the flaming sword of William the Conqueror." An accumulation on these lines, though not without interest, can hardly be considered a collection in the true sense, because there has been no proper selection or discrimination.

Quite often a collection begins in a very casual way. Odd pieces of pottery are acquired on holiday either at home or abroad, perhaps after seeing the articles actually produced. We tell our friends about these, and often as a result other pieces are received as gifts. Interest is stimulated; knowledge grows; and systematic buying begins.

The Character of the Collector

A good collector has to have a combination of special qualities. It is a great advantage if, to begin with, he has good taste in artistic matters, for this seems to be something with which fortunate individuals are born. Granted this particular kind of perception and instinct, a man is not yet a collector unless he also has enthusiasm and enjoys the game for its own sake: some people with impeccable taste feel no inclination to collect. Then again determination and perseverance are needed, for a worthwhile collection cannot be formed hurriedly or without the exercise of a good deal of patience.

Having a flair for collecting provides the foundation, but we still have to build on it if we are to progress very far. The collector is bound to have some more or less painful experiences, but these play their part in helping to form mature judgment. One way of avoiding mistakes, however, is to take every opportunity of studying public or private collections of ceramics.

It gives point to a summer excursion if a visit is to be paid to a notable collection in an art gallery or museum, in some mansion open to the public or, as regards contemporary work, in the showrooms of leading stores or even in works studios. This hobby should not be confined to the British Isles. If the collector is fortunate enough to have a holiday abroad, the chance of seeing and comparing foreign pieces with our own can be most valuable.

The Choice of China

Almost any field open to the collector proves to be vast upon close acquaintance, and the need for specialisation early becomes evident. In pottery there is an almost infinite range and choice, which probably explains why it has so long held first place in the affections of collectors. One may decide to concentrate on ancient pottery or upon examples of the most modern fashion. Geography may be taken as the basis, and a collection formed of pottery from Corinth, Corsica or Copenhagen. We may select pots for their beauty of form or colour, or may deliberately disregard the aesthetic side and collect the cooking pots of African tribes because of the way they illustrate folk customs. We may decide that our interest lies in the products of a particular factory or of a maker who gained a reputation for a certain kind of ware. Or again the attraction may be in collecting the pottery covers of pomade jars, heraldic china, tavern ale pots, the figures of shepherdesses and the like, ornamental pot door knobs and finger-plates, or anything else that happens to take our fancy.

Quality Counts

To collect more or less at random to begin with does no harm so long as it is not allowed to develop into a habit. It is useful in enabling us to find out where our main interest lies, what kinds of pottery are available from local dealers and other sources, and the pieces that are within comfortable reach of our purse. But it follows that when we have adopted one line we should be prepared to discard the others.

It is quite normal to have brought together a fair number of miscellaneous pieces before it becomes clear that we must specialise, if only because of lack of house-room. This may well be regarded as an inevitable stage in our training, just as a general education is necessary before a profession is chosen.

Some undiscriminating people with magpie tendencies seem to place quantity before quality, and will buy cracked pots, ones that have been broken and roughly mended with rivets, or figure subjects that have limbs missing. It is, of course, tempting even for the expert to have imperfect pieces to illustrate special features when better ones are not to be come by, but much the wisest course in ordinary circumstances is to put quality first.

A great deal of fun can be got out of collecting some small and humble object that costs very little, and as long as we are breaking new ground, which is not nearly so difficult as one might think, it is doing a public service to preserve specimens. The collector who is both bold and wealthy may prefer, on the other hand, to establish his reputation by means of a few very choice and costly pieces of great rarity that are among the best of their kind.

Fakes and Forgeries

Much could be said about the hazards which face the collector of pottery or porcelain in following his hobby, and forgeries are one of the things against which he has to be constantly on his guard. The circumstances in which ceramic forgeries are found vary greatly and, as some early records show, are by no means confined to modern times.

Sometimes forgers give themselves away by the limitations of their own knowledge. Thus upon occasion they have put the mark of one early factory on a product that could only have been made at quite a different one, or have used a mark confined to certain years on pots of a design belonging to another period. But in other cases the details of the reproduction have been so carefully studied that even experts have been misled.

In the past, forgers have not infrequently been encouraged by purchasers who have not themselves been entirely blameless. The late W. B. Honey mentions a piece with an incorrect date and markings which he says was probably supplied to gratify the passion of the well-known collector Robert Drana for important, unique and historic pieces.

Nowadays a certain amount of critical knowledge about

pottery and porcelain is more common than at any time in the past. Public collections in museums and art galleries have been greatly extended and are now often displayed so attractively that they arouse increasing interest and attention in visitors. In the same way the cabinets of beautiful porcelain available for viewing in so many country houses play their part in making information more readily available. One of the good effects of this has been to make collectors more cautious about doubtful attributions.

Museum curators and art gallery directors are tolerant people and can give most valuable advice if you are doubtful about the authenticity of any of your treasured pieces. There are so many ways in which forgeries betray themselves. To the eye of the expert the hard brightness of modern material lacks the fine natural patina or surface mellowing that comes with age and use. The script of markings or dates of the various famous factories are as familiar to the specialist as the handwriting of intimate friends, so that crude copies are at once revealed in their true light. And even in difficult cases the comparison of established pieces with others can show many subtle differences.

The best defence against fakes and forgeries is to collect for the love of the thing. Collecting solely as an investment can be richly rewarding but has its dangers. Because Chinese porcelain fetches high prices in world markets, it has been "reproduced" in Paris. In such circumstances avarice can lead to costly mistakes. But if a man loves what is beautiful he comes to appreciate the aesthetic qualities of the pieces he collects, and as he becomes increasingly aware of the rhythm and delicacy of the modelling and colour of his porcelain, he becomes more likely to purchase wisely.

Records of Purchases

When buying your pieces of Chelsea, Derby or Worcester ware it is well to persuade the dealer to give a receipted invoice on which the purchase is described. It may be necessary to overcome a good deal of reluctance, because if anything that has been stated is untrue a legitimate claim can be made, and such accounts should be preserved as evidence in case of a resale. As an additional safeguard, and for convenience of reference, it is worth making a copy of the details in a record book or on a card index. The latter has the advantage that it can easily be kept up to date when changes are made in the collection.

Another way in which records can be extremely useful is as a reminder of where purchases of particular types of ware were made. When a collection is growing it will often be found that some pieces can be duplicated quite easily; that some can only be traced after the expenditure of a great deal of time and trouble; but that there will remain odd ones needed to complete a representative series which it appears no amount of patience will enable you to find. In such cases to look through lists and invoices can be very rewarding.

It is, of course, a pleasant exercise to consult your records and documents because they will bring vividly to mind the happy occasions when you bought some of your most treasured possessions. You will be reminded of exploring the quiet by-ways of some old town, the unexpected discovery of one or more antique shops with real objects to sell instead of the usual rubbish, your chat with the antique dealer himself, who proved himself so knowledgeable and informative, and the leisurely inspection of the stock and the buying of a few delightful pieces at very reasonable cost.

The author has had this kind of experience at places as far apart as Hexham, near the Northumbrian moors;

Knutsford in Cheshire, the original of Mrs. Gaskell's
Cranford and of Barrie's *Quality Street*, with porcelain
displayed to great advantage in an elegant Georgian house;
the ancient city of Lincoln, where a stiff climb up the
narrow streets leading to the Cathedral was richly repaid
by what was discovered in one of the shops there; St.
Albans, only half an hour from the City of London but
with all the atmosphere of a country town in an agricultural
area; and Woodstock, a sleepy little place just outside the
park of Blenheim Palace with some choice pieces in more
than one excellent antique shop.

If at the time such visits are made, the exact names and
addresses of shops are noted down, with some brief details
of the kinds of pottery and porcelain dealt in, one can
communicate with them readily and know which can be
consulted most fruitfully when special needs arise. To be
systematic will save anyone time, and good records are
essential for those of us whose memories, perhaps many
years after a town was visited, are not above reproach.
The joy of seeing the tantalising gap filled at last makes well
worth while all the pains taken and frustrations suffered.

Rockingham Ware

Probably the most desirable quality in a collector is good
taste, though it is not always present. This will be evident
if we refer briefly to the history of Rockingham ware,
which unfortunately is typical of a number that could be
chosen. The porcelain in question was made at the York-
shire village of Swinton, on the estate of the Marquis of
Rockingham, in the first half of the 19th century.

The works first became prosperous by producing modest
brown teapots and the like, and could well have continued
to make this kind of pottery successfully. From about
1820, however, Thomas Brameld, one of the proprietors,
began to take an interest in porcelain, backed by the

119

financial support of Lord Rockingham. By 1823 the technical difficulties of making a good bone china appeared to have been overcome, and full-scale manufacture of the new product was begun. A large amount of money was spent, but the optimism shown proved premature, and in 1825 a meeting of creditors was called.

Rockingham, already involved, was a man of great wealth and decided to take full financial responsibility, while continuing to employ Brameld as the practical manager. There then began an extraordinary era during which the works turned out costly and gorgeous ornamental pieces and dessert services which were "absolutely bereft of the most elementary notions of design, colour and decorative effects." The pieces were encrusted with paintings and ornament in deplorable taste. One vase, now in the Victoria and Albert Museum, is painted with scenes from the history of Don Quixote, "supplemented with medallions of landscapes and birds, flowers and scrolls, distributed upon all available space." The vase stands upon lion's claws and is surmounted by a rhinoceros, making up what indeed was a "nonsensical agglomeration."

Appalling products of the kind mentioned found a ready market among people who should have known better. The Duchess of Cumberland paid 250 guineas for a Rockingham dessert service, when money was worth several times what it is now, and the Duke of Sussex ordered one costing 850 guineas. Others went to the crowned heads of Europe. Finally, William IV ordered a dessert service for which £5,000 was paid and which was first used at the coronation of Queen Victoria. This transaction caused the factory to adopt the style of the " Royal Rockingham Works." The set was painted with the Royal arms, views of English castles, and landscape scenery in unpleasant, lurid colours that were completely false to nature.

In spite of ready sales and high prices, costs were

ruinously high. The chief painter, who received a stiff fee for each piece he decorated, appears to have had no qualifications for the job beyond his being the brother of Brameld, the manager. In the circumstances it is not surprising that Rockingham lost so much money that in 1842 he closed the works.

The Lowestoft Tradition

Even the very experienced collector often finds it hard to be sure about the origin of the pieces in his cabinet, for the elements of doubt and obscurity may be great. Reference to one such case will serve to show the circumstances that can arise.

When Chaffers was collecting material for his work *Marks and Monograms on Pottery and Porcelain,* of which the first edition was published in 1863, he visited Lowestoft and found in the neighbourhood numerous pieces of porcelain which had long been in the possession of leading local families, and were marked with their crests or monograms. The tradition was that all this pottery had been made in the district, but with so many specimens surviving this would have indicated manufacture on quite an extensive scale, and the evidence could show nothing beyond a very small establishment with extremely limited output. How could these conflicting features be reconciled?

Investigation in more recent years has shown that in the mid-18th century the local pottery works began to supplement their manufacturing business by acting as merchants for blue and white Delft faience. This was convenient because the geographical position of the town lent itself to trade with Holland by way of Yarmouth. Once this trade was established it grew rapidly and extended in directions which were not foreseen, one of the first changes being that the importing of soft porcelain was added to that of faience.

An interesting complication that arose in the second half of the 18th century was that a high proportion of the porcelain which came to Lowestoft from Holland was not of Dutch but of Chinese origin. The whole position was extraordinarily intricate, for the trade in faience continued side by side with that of porcelain, and at least as regards the former it appears that local shipowners carried English clay and the raw materials to Holland and brought back pottery which was badged and inscribed at home.

There is still another aspect of the business to be noted. The East India Company was incorporated to develop trade with India and the Far East, being founded towards the end of the 16th century to compete with Dutch merchants who were already well established in these markets. The Company enjoyed great prosperity, and was granted a royal charter by Queen Elizabeth I on 31st December, 1600. It continued its very extensive operations until superseded by the British Government in 1858.

The activities of the East India Company might appear very remote from those of Lowestoft, but in practice this was not so. There was very lively competition with the Dutch. The East India Company had the monopoly of an extremely valuable trade with China, chiefly in tea, and charged high prices at home. If a proportion of Chinese porcelain was included in consignments from Holland there was no need for the authorities to be any the wiser, while good profits could be earned by circumventing the monopoly. It will be evident, however, that the nature of the trade made it somewhat confidential.

So for one reason or another these Lowestoft wares might be almost anything: although sold by the local pottery they were very often from the Continent or the Orient. All of which goes to show that it is unwise to be dogmatic about attributions and origins.

Collecting Pots as the Witch-Doctor does Skulls

There is an interesting point of view about collecting to which reference should be made. Essentially, it is that as pottery is intimately associated with our daily lives, we should not divorce the two even so far as collecting is concerned.

One aspect of this thesis is that, even if a man has a cabinet full of fine ornamental china, he is not a real enthusiast if he uses only common earthenware at the breakfast table. If he really cared enough about it, we may say, he would so abhor the inferior article that he would not give it house-room. And many cultured people do in fact make regular use of lovely domestic china, who would not for a moment regard themselves as collectors. Yet they are very worthy members of the fraternity, with their collection based on use and not just on display.

A more subtle aspect is that objects need to be in their natural setting for full aesthetic appreciation. We may consider that we get more pleasure from elegant china-ware on the tea-table, taking its place among the silver and napery, than we do from a score of antique teapots on the shelves of a cabinet.

It is even held that there is something barbarous in hoarding things together, and in putting pots on shelves like the rows of skulls in the hut of an African witch-doctor. Certainly it is a moving experience to visit a collection like that of the *Musée de Cluny* at Paris where, in a superb architectural setting, all kinds of treasures in the way of rich furnishings, paintings and porcelain are shown in their appropriate relationship to each other.

If we keep strictly to the rule of buying a vase only when we have just the right niche for it, we are unlikely to acquire a very extensive collection. But if we have a keen eye for objects of beauty, the few pieces of pottery with which we ornament our home will help to create an atmos-

123

phere of culture and good taste, often at very modest cost.

Chinese Horsemen in Derbyshire

Even stern limiting of purchases does not necessarily prohibit collecting as usually understood: we can still collect while limiting ourselves to pieces that are in keeping with the surroundings we have available. A whitewashed Cornish cottage, often filled with sunlight, may be just right for gay pieces of contemporary studio pottery, while for a flat in the West End something more sophisticated may be required.

The exciting thing to realise is that we can exercise our individual tastes and preferences so as to achieve something that has never been done before. As an example of this may be mentioned the collection of porcelain at Hardwick Hall in Derbyshire. Included in this collection are a few very choice specimens of Chinese horsemen. The colour splendour of these figures finds a perfect background in the neutral grey of stone walls, and the spaciousness of the great mansion ensures that each work is completely isolated. So oriental art finds a unique setting in the Derbyshire countryside, with aesthetic results that are deeply satisfying.

Care of Curios

Collecting is a very civilised custom, and one which yields great cultural and educational value to its devotees. There is also the point that, but for the activities of collectors and the dealers who serve them, countless specimens would be lost to posterity. Such loss would include most valuable artistic and technical knowledge. So the community is very much indebted to the collector.

At the same time the ownership of beautiful objects of fine craftsmanship, representing some of the highest achievements of human thought and skill, is not to be treated lightly. It is a heavy responsibility to have in our possession pottery which may be centuries old and which cannot be replaced: it is our duty to take good care of it.

Knocks are so easily given to pottery displayed in the open that a cabinet, or series of cabinets, is a necessity. The use of these has the additional advantage of reducing very greatly the amount of cleaning that is required so that, instead of attention being given every few days, once in six months may prove sufficient.

From the point of view of safety it is undesirable to clean pottery more often than is strictly necessary, for accidents are most often liable to happen while the pieces are being handled, either through bumps or falls. Some simple precautions are necessary while the work is being done. It is a good thing to place a rubber mat in the bowl being used for washing the pieces, although if this is not handy a towel may be made to serve the same purpose.

A point of great importance, which cannot be too strongly emphasised, is that the water must only be slightly warmed to hardly more than tepid, for really hot water very often removes gilding and paint, besides dissolving and disintegrating some of the basic materials. It is not desirable to add soda to the water, because this quickly affects the colours, and this applies to any of the stronger chemical compositions which are now on the market. Often water alone is sufficient to do the job, but if anything else is needed it should be limited to a little soft soap of good quality.

Washing Whatnots

Apart from soap and water we require only a brush with bristles that are soft and long enough to enter all crevices. The very knowledgable collector Percy Haigh recommends the use of a shaving-brush as being ideal for the purpose, and the larger type well filled with badger bristles does the work quickly with no danger to the ornaments.

It is convenient to have a second bowl of water into which the pieces can be dipped to remove the soapy film after treatment. All that then remains is to let them drain until dry, for there is risk in anything like hard rubbing; a light final polishing when the pottery is already dry, and then only with a soft clean cloth, is all that should be permitted.

Cleaning makes a big difference to the attractiveness of pottery. When the pieces sparkle we can appreciate more fully the excellence of the porcelain or other substance. After washing, the colour harmonies stand out more vividly and richly, and the complete details of the design and decoration are clearly revealed. The pleasure to be derived from our collection is enhanced if there is evidence that it is cherished.

The Display Cabinet

The cabinet itself should not be forgotten. To be worthy of the treasures it holds it is preferable that it should be a handsome piece of furniture, well designed for display purposes, and made from rich woods. It should be soundly constructed so as to be dustproof, and should have doors that open easily without jolting the contents. It should stand firmly, so that the vibration of passing footsteps and the like does not cause precious pieces to move about. It should be kept immaculate, with well-polished windows and no dusty corners. The best results cannot be obtained without a good deal of trouble and outlay.

12

COLLECTORS' CURIOS

Dabbities and Doggies of the 17th century—Pottery Chargers for Salome and Charles II—Armorial Drug Jars—Punch Bowls and Soup Tureens for City Livery Companies—Crests and Coronets on Dinner Services ornamented by Chinese Heraldic Artists—Collecting "Long Elizas"—Buccaros Bowls of scented clay from Central America.

Dabbities and Doggies

In the days of our grandparents many cottage homes had a pair of china dogs, or a dog and cat, on either end of the chimney-piece in the sitting-room. These figures were also to be found in farm kitchens, and were sometimes offered as prizes at country fairs. Although crudely moulded they were gay with their white, red and gold colouring, and were larger than most pottery ornaments.

At first sight such objects might appear to be beneath the notice of the serious collector of curios, but in fact they represent a very ancient tradition, and therefore have much of interest about them. In Scotland, for instance, a merchant named John Bonyman who died in 1631, had among his effects "thrie lame babies and thrie lame doggies." If we interpret this we find that actually he left not sadly afflicted children, but "loam" or earthenware "dabbities" or toy figures, together with similar models of dogs.

If we go a little farther back we find that in 1562 the possessions left by Mary Queen of Scots included "ane figure of ane doig," in pottery, and that this was said to

127

have come from Spain. The dogs were in fact originally Spanish, being made there by Moorish potters, who in turn derived their craft from Persian potters of many centuries earlier.

So our china "doggies," although perhaps crude enough to-day, find a very respectable ancestry in the gorgeous ware of Persia long ago. In the same way china cats are also of long descent. In Egypt, where cats were regarded as sacred, representations of them were made in clay, and some of these models were found in the tomb of Tutankhamen.

If we are at all curious about our treasures it is often the case that there is more to them than meets the eye. China dogs and cats may appear the most commonplace articles, yet as we have seen they have their background, and this is the rule rather than the exception. In other words the collector is usually justified in his enthusiasm for his curios, as research into their history can be fascinating.

Pottery Chargers for Salome and Charles II

A certain bloodthirsty lady named Salome, when offered a reward for her dancing, asked that the head of a gentleman named John should be presented to her on a charger. The word "charger" in this case means not a warhorse but "a large flat dish or platter for carrying meat." The flat shape and spacious dimensions of a pottery charger make it suitable for scenic and other decoration, and in consequence we sometimes find it among collectors' curios.

A collection of English tin-enamelled chargers was formed by G. F. Denny. Some of these were auctioned at Sotheby's in 1956, and one of them in English Delft, $6\frac{1}{2}$ inches in diameter, painted in blue, brown, green and yellow, sold for £1,550. This charger, dated 1668, showed the pleasure yacht of Charles II, presented to him at the Restoration by the Dutch Government. The piece was contemporary,

Made of fine earthenware these vases and carafes are hand painted by the Delft or in-glaze technique or diffused colours. *By courtesy of Carter, Stabler and Adams Ltd.*

(*Upper*) This attractive service features the "Burgundy" pattern. Although the design is fairly traditional, the effect is still one of modern elegance. *By courtesy of Doulton Fine China Ltd.*
(*Lower*) This delightful example of modern pottery is called "Jamaica." The almost childlike simplicity of the design is carried out in bold colours. *By courtesy of Joseph Bourne & Son Ltd.*

as the yacht was mentioned by Pepys shortly before the charger was made.

Armorial Drug Jars

A rare Lambeth delft drug jar was sold at Sotheby's in 1955 for £215. It was painted with the arms of the City of London on the base, while the swelling body part carried the arms, supporters and crest of the Worshipful Society of Apothecaries together with masses of heraldic mantling, the whole being highly decorative.

A drug jar of this kind was designed for utility, and part of the aesthetic pleasure derived from it is because we appreciate its fitness for purpose as well as its good shape. There is, however, the reminder that our ancestors had the enviable attitude of mind which caused them to be willing to devote skill, time and money to the embellishment of articles intended for common use. The workaday jar becomes an art treasure to us both because it is so pleasant to look at and because we have lost something of this faculty.

Punch Bowls and Soup Tureens

A small but choice collection of pottery and porcelain bearing arms of the livery companies of the City of London was made early in the present century by F. A. Crisp, a Fellow of the Society of Antiquaries. He left it to the nation and it is now to be seen in the London Museum at Lancaster House.

A feature of the collection, as one might expect, is the large punch bowls, more or less essential to the convivial evenings of our ancestors. The other items, too, are all connected with food and drink, including soup tureens, large plates and dishes, jugs and mugs, and ceremonial salts. A rather surprising thing is that there are several part or complete tea services, for one does not visualise the liverymen making much use of teapots and milk jugs at their formal gatherings. Perhaps, however, the Court of Assistants may sometimes have had tea served to refresh them after their deliberations.

As regards period, a number of examples are from the 17th century, the remainder mainly from the following century. It would be interesting to know to what extent the Livery Companies are acquiring armorial china to-day, for it is certainly gaining increasing recognition elsewhere. Shortly after the Second World War, the City of Manchester had presented to it an extensive service of fine china bearing the civic coat-of-arms, with the cost shared among the Aldermen and Councillors.

The coat-of-arms shown are very picturesque and usually have a bearing on the ancient craft of the livery company concerned. Thus the Blacksmiths' Company shows hammers; the Brewers have barrels and a mermaid with dishevelled hair holding in her outstretched hands ears of barley; the Butchers have slaughter axes and bulls' heads; the Poulterers show storks, swans and pelicans; the Fishmongers have dolphins; and the Cutlers show magnificent swords with blades of silver and hilts and pommels of gold.

Crests and Coronets

Evidence of the curious bypaths taken by international trade are often to be found in the saleroom. One such case is that of 18th-century dinner services made in China but with English armorial bearings. To enable copies of these to be made, the coats-of-arms, crests or coronets were sent out and were copied quite faithfully.

For a period the imports of this kind of ware by noble and county families were large, and hundreds of the sets still survive. While heraldic badging makes a discrete and elegant form of decoration it is a little surprising that private purchasers can be found for china bearing the arms of families with which they have no connection, although the same thing happens with antique silverware.

Purchases for public collections are naturally quite a different matter, and a number of our museums and art galleries have been enriched in this way. A case in point is that of the Bowes Museum at Barnard Castle. Among the many fine ceramic items there shown, is a wide range of this 18th-century Chinese porcelain, bearing the coats-of-arms of the Bowes and other British families, together with other sets ornamented with the armorials of families in other parts of Europe on whose orders they were executed. One reason for the international flavour in this collection is that the founder, the Hon. John Bowes, a son of the 10th Earl of Strathmore, had a residence in Paris and married Josephine Benoite, Countess Montalbo.

Some of these heraldic plates had well authenticated adventures before finally reaching the saleroom. There was a plate from a service made in China for Lord Archibald Hamilton, son of the third Duke, about the year 1720, and on his death in 1754 the service passed to Sir William Hamilton, then our Ambassador at Naples. A single plate from this set was sold in London in 1956 for £90.

The Chinese Heraldic Artist
It was far from easy for the Chinese artist to decorate armorial porcelain correctly, and one of the features of great interest to the curio collector is to observe the errors that occur. When birds appear on the coats-of-arms, for example, the Chinese versions are apt to be so different from the conventional European heraldic ones that it becomes difficult to identify them, so that the arms may be assigned to the wrong family.

This is not to say that the Chinese were not painstakingly thorough. In one service the customer's instructions had been so carefully noted that under the shield on every piece were the words: " There are the arms of myself and my wife," with the neat original script accurately reproduced. Sometimes, of course, the handwriting of the patron could not be so easily read, as in the case of the family whose motto was interpreted as " Stink and Stank," instead of " Think and Thank."

In general, however, the mistakes were not numerous considering the absence of direct contact between buyer and seller. Perhaps the commonest one was misinterpretation of the heraldic tinctures when the artist was working, say, from an engraved book-plate in which the colours were indicated only by the recognised system of vertical, horizontal and other lines. The conventions of heraldry are often sufficiently subtle to mystify those who are not expert in their study. One basic rule that was transgressed in China was that there should not be a charge of metal upon metal, or colour upon colour. How was the artist to know that he could not place a gold chevron on a silver field, although it might be perfectly correct for the chevron to be red, blue, green, or some other colour? Or how was he to be aware that a blackbird could appear against a gold background but must not venture into a green field? However disconcerting such blunders might be to the proud owners when they first unpacked the service, they do not in any way lessen the decorative quality of the pieces to-day.

Among the pieces of armorial porcelain of the 18th century illustrated by Tudor-Craig in his book on the subject, are some forming part of a service made for Colonel John Chadwick (1720-1800), of Healey Hall, Lancashire. The porcelain was made at Ching-tê-Chên and travelled many hundreds of miles by river and mountain pass before reaching the coast at Canton. Here the ware was painted with the coats-of-arms, for at this time Canton was an important centre of foreign trade, as ships had the right to anchor, and merchants were allowed to trade ashore at the "hongs" on the waterfront. There were numerous enamelling establishments which kept in close touch with foreign merchants.

Tudor-Craig shows that armorial porcelain was produced almost entirely between 1700 and 1820. After the latter date there was hardly any call for the oriental product, as the Worcester factory had firmly established this type of manufacture at home. There were more than three generations within the hundred and twenty years mentioned and some families had several services made for them, with heraldic differences of considerable interest. The Roberts family, for example, had its first service made for the head of the family in 1735, another for the son in 1780, and a third for the granddaughter about 1795, the arms shown indicating the alliances made by marriage in the period.

Collecting " Long Elizas "

The blue and white porcelain of the K'ang-Hai period, well-known to collectors, is noteworthy for the scenes painted upon it, including figures, landscapes, flowers, birds and animals. The Willow Pattern is an anglicised version of one such subject, but there are many others. Some ginger jars in this kind of ware have the whole surface covered with scenes of boys playing games. Another type of blue and white vase, slender and high-shouldered with a knobbed cover, carries the tall and graceful figures of *mei yén*, or pretty girls. Dutch importers nicknamed these " Lang Lijsen," a term which subsequently became anglicised as " Long Elizas."

Opportunities for collecting can sometimes be found in unexpected places. An unusual example is that of the collection of Chinese export porcelain presented to the British Museum in 1853 by H. Adams. All the specimens had been recovered from old wrecks of East Indiamen found in Table Bay, in what was then Cape Colony. The range of wares salvaged by Adams in this way is extensive, and the circumstances enable the pieces to be dated fairly accurately which, as we know, is often a difficult thing to do. It seems strange that the Museum should benefit from a hobby based on misfortune at sea.

Buccaros Bowls of Scented Clay

A ceramic curiosity of an extraordinary kind was the scented pottery of remote parts of Central America. The clay from which this product of the American Indians was made had the characteristic of being impregnated with an attractive natural perfume.

The pieces were first imported into Europe by the Portuguese and a strong demand for them sprang up in the Iberian Peninsula and in Italy. In addition to their excellent shape and ornamentation, they were highly esteemed because, coming from areas where few travellers penetrated, they were to begin with rare and costly.

A special interest in these so-called "noble buccaros" arose because collectors began to ascribe wonderful virtues to them. Thus if linen soaked in water held in a buccaros bowl were applied to the forehead of a patient suffering from a burning fever, the fever would soon abate. Broken pieces were mounted in gold and carried as charms.

The effect was specially strong if the buccaros was consumed, being thought capable, for example, of turning a negro into a white man if he ate it at the proper time. It became the custom, particularly in Italy and Spain, for pieces of vases and the like to be ground to a fine powder for introduction into sweetmeats or for being formed into small lozenges. It came about, therefore, that by the early 18th century buccaros-eating was being "immoderately indulged in," and Dr. Daniel Geyers of Dresden, in a pamphlet published in 1735, gives an account of the consequences suffered by a lady who ate a whole cup and saucer at one go!

Once a demand on a fair scale had arisen, as in this case, it was natural for supply to be stimulated, and buccaros production was considerably expanded. At Natan, a small town near Panama, black ones continued to be made by the aboriginal tribes, but manufacture was begun elsewhere. Santiago, the capital of Chile, became the main centre of supply, and the monks of four monasteries there depended for their maintenance entirely upon its manufacture. Gaudalajara in Mexico earned a reputation for buccaros which were especially highly scented, and imitations came to be made to a limited extent even in Portugal. In view of all this activity it is remarkable that no genuine examples of buccaros appear to have survived.

13

POTTERY PRICES

Collecting as an investment—The relationship of the art-lover and the speculative purchaser—The comparison of prices at different periods—The effect of rarity on prices and some examples of high figures realised at auctions—Sales of English pieces from Bow, Chelsea, Derby, Staffordshire and Worcester—Continental porcelain, with particular reference to Dresden, Sèvres and Nymphenburg—Porcelain of the Orient.

Collecting as an Investment

It is best to be disinterested about collecting, because otherwise it is easy to stray on to some very unsafe ground, like the rich man who would only buy pictures by Royal Academicians but never bought a good painting. At the same time, the collector of pottery is naturally very much concerned with the value of the pieces he acquires.

Cost is an important factor when deciding what types to collect. The interest and pleasure to be derived from bringing together modestly priced pieces may be just as great as anything the very wealthy man gets from his treasures, but the range of our purse has to be taken into account when making our choice.

Collecting has many facets. One of the invigorating things about the hobby is that we back our judgment against the world. We may consider that the figure subjects modelled by a young and unknown man or woman of the present day have special merit, and that they are so pleasing to us that we wish to collect them. If they really are exceptionally good, and if we have been pioneers in discovering this, the amount we invest may eventually be multiplied many times over.

The true art-lover buys for his own pleasure, or to increase his own knowledge, and being swayed comparatively little by fashion, he tends to remain on safe ground. The man gambling for the sake of gain, or the credulous folk who buy on the top of the market, are much more likely to be landed with a cartload of junk. In pottery and porcelain, as in other art-forms, there are many examples of large fluctuations in value between periods.

When really high prices are paid for works of art the interesting question arises of how permanent the values may be. Very ancient and beautiful things of established reputation can become almost priceless, so that in a sense any figure offered is a nominal one. On the other hand with lesser pieces fashion may enhance prices less soundly.

It has commonly been remarked that rarity as well as quality has a ruling influence on the price of old china, and it is easy to see how this situation arises. When porcelain was first made in England the number of pieces produced was very limited, so that a high proportion of those that have survived, especially those of artistic merit, have now found their way into leading public or private collections. If, therefore, the amateur wishes to secure a respresentative specimen of what is still available he has to pay stiffly for it.

In general all the factors of change favour the serious collector. If a collection is made with taste and discrimination and held for a number of years it is almost bound to rise in value, probably very substantially. The fact that money is worth less and less has the result that prices of antique pottery and porcelain are continually being moved upwards.

More subtle though equally significant influences are at work. Thus craftsmanship, even in the making of decorative ceramic ware, has been largely superseded by the factory production line, so that anything that has been made by hand is becoming more and more of a rarity in the modern world, even when allowance is made for the often delightful, but always very limited, replacements of our artistic stock made by the studio potters of to-day. And, apart from the gradual deterioration of age, accidents do happen, so that breakage increases scarcity.

Although ceramics are put up for auction very frequently, there usually seems to be a steady demand for any pieces that have real merit or interest. At one of the regular sales of Sotheby's held early in November, 1962, a total of £14,328 was obtained for various items of continental pottery and porcelain, the English dealers finding themselves faced with severe competition from several European countries. Later in the same month Sotheby's sold a collection of Ming porcelain, owned by Mr. and Mrs. R. H. R. Palmer, for £50,748. Some details of individual items will be given later.

High prices have not developed suddenly: the process is one which already has a long history and which continues to-day. Over half a century ago Solon recorded the sale of a teapot from a set made in Bristol porcelain in 1774, with form and decorations taken from Dresden models. This teapot, sold by itself, found a purchaser at £210. Such a price for such a humble article may appear remarkable, and must have been many times the original cost of manufacture. If the same piece were offered in the saleroom to-day, however, the old price would no doubt be made to look very modest indeed.

Auctions of ceramics are held frequently in the rooms of such famous old firms as Christie's (otherwise Christie, Manson & Woods Ltd., of St. James's Place, London, S.W.1, founded in 1766), or Sotheby's (otherwise Sotheby & Co., of New Bond Street, London, W.1.). Besides these leading English establishments there is the Hotel Drouot in Paris, and the Parke-Bernet Galleries of Madison Avenue, New York, where important sales of pottery and porcelain also take place from time to time. Prices realised are reported in *The Times*, in a number of the leading monthly journals, and in the annual *Art Prices Current*.

To a remarkable extent London keeps the lead as the chief art centre of the world. Perhaps one reason is that Britain is a kind of half-way house between the Continent and the United States. Whatever the reason, Dutch, German, French and other buyers as well as American come and compete actively against each other at London auctions of ceramics. English specimens of pottery and porcelain maintain a good steady market, though Continental pieces may reach much more spectacular figures, and Oriental pieces sometimes reach the highest prices of all.

Sales of English Pieces

Of English ceramics several scores of each of the famous makes find their way into the saleroom every year. It is instructive to examine the figures, for when taken over a period they provide a sensitive gauge of values. Probably prices are decided chiefly by the informed opinion of professional antique dealers, but the market is certainly influenced also by amateur purchasers buying for the excellent reason that a particular piece appeals to them.

Of Bow porcelain in one year recently prices ranged from £40 to £50 for modest pieces up to £2,000 or more for exceptional ones. At Sotheby's in 1950 a figure of Harlequin made at this factory, after a Meissen original by Kandler, brought £1,700—no mean price for a copy! In this case Harlequin, in his tradition brightly coloured costume, is shown sitting on a tree-stump, playing a pipe held in his left hand, while with his right he holds a monkey.

139

Another Harlequin, sold on the same occasion for £1,200, shows him with a wide-open mouth and ribald expression, holding a pug dog under his left arm, and turning its tail as though the dog were a hurdy-gurdy. In the same year a pair of Bow parrots, with brilliant plumage in black, green, blue and yellow, were sold in the same rooms for £2,000. Porcelain lends itself well to subjects such as this, in which the colouring can be gay but at the same time delicate and charming.

Chelsea porcelain is even more highly esteemed. Prices from £100 to £200 are common, and there have been several recent instances in the range between £2,000 and £5,000 for quite small and simple objects. Two little hawk owls, in reddish-brown, yellow and grey were sold at Sotheby's for £3,200. A white owl on an oak-stump, with its left claw grasping a dead mouse, brought £3,400, while a pair of swans, 5 in. and 4¾ in. high, with cygnets, after Meissen originals, brought £4,400.

Natural history subjects are great favourites, especially birds or other creatures which can be depicted with their appealing young in lifelike fashion. A variant of this is the owl and mouse just mentioned, which again gives the ceramic artist an opportunity of showing how vivid realism can be achieved in his medium. But other subjects are not uncommon, so that we find a figure described as a "Chelsea Lady from Italian Comedy" reaching £2,050, but William Augustus, Duke of Cumberland, going for a mere £95.

Prices of Derby porcelain are comparatively moderate, mainly between £40 and £50, while just a few items achieve the £400 to £700 range. At Sotheby's a hurdy-gurdy after Carl van Loo went for £410, while £640 was paid for an attractive group of the four seasons, after Meissen originals by Eberlein. The figures, 8¾ in. to 9½ in. high, comprise a woman in a flowered dress holding a nosegay in her left hand for Spring; a woman with a wheatsheaf at her side for Summer; Bacchus leaning on a tree-trunk eating grapes, with an infant satyr sitting beside him on a barrel, for Autumn; and an old man with a brazier and a *putto* chopping wood, for Winter.

Staffordshire items are fairly numerous, but do not fetch high prices. Cow milk jugs sell for £20 to £40; Pratt figures of a bear and a lion sold recently for £40 and £54 respectively; while an Enoch Wood lost sheep brought £44, and a Ralph Wood spaniel £40.

Worcester ware, which is often very colourful, is supported well in both American and English salerooms. In the 1950's an important set of three Worcester vases, of the Dr. Wall period and with equestrian decoration, went together for £1,260, or an average of £420 each. The centre vase showed a horse being shod; the side vases had in one case a horseman taking refreshment outside an inn, and in the other an equestrian figure with a peasant woman in a landscape scene. In 1961 a rare Worcester junket dish mould with scallop shell ornament realised £520, and an apple-green sauce-tureen with stand and cover £540, while a mug dated 1754 brought £720. In the same year a Worcester basket 11 in. wide with pierced sides and twig handles sold for £150, while a set of three of these with a yellow ground made £490 and a pair with covers and stands, £540.

Contrasts in prices for the same type of ware can sometimes be very remarkable. A Worcester service of forty pieces, for instance, offered at Sotheby's in March, 1956, brought £300, or £7 odd a piece. Yet in the following May, at the same rooms, a rare Worcester yellow-scale teapot made £1,000, a record figure, and smaller items from the same service also sold well, a teacup and saucer bringing £200, a coffee cup and saucer £240, and a milk jug £320. Prices like this soon mount up, and at the latter sale the

English pottery and porcelain sold in a single day realised a total of £9,303.

Continental Porcelain

Antique Continental porcelain undoubtedly finds its main market in London. The French, however, are specially interested in what they themselves have made, and Sèvres pieces are often offered in Paris. We have less of a monopoly, too, in Dresden china, which sells well in New York.

One of the largest sums for Copenhagen china in the past few years was £1,312 paid at Christie's for a dinner service of the late 18th century, painted with birds, fruit, flowers and landscapes.

The prices of Dresden china have mainly been between £40 and £100. One fine table group which brought £94 showed Venus seated in a chariot drawn by three swans, and holding an apple in one hand, with Cupid at her side assisting in the driving. Knight, Frank & Rutley of London sold a Dresden 21-branch chandelier of 75 lights for £493 10s. in 1950. About this time too, there were several sales of Dresden china at the Parke-Bernet Galleries in New York. Tea services sold for $100 to $200; dessert services from $200 to $400; and dinner services from $700 to $900.

In Meissen ware figures by J. J. Kändler are the highlights. In December, 1950, Sotheby's sold a cock and hen with white egg for £1,600. Parrots brought £480 to £620 apiece. In November of the same year Christie's secured £840 for a pair of cats, each with a paw raised, and one of them with a mouse in its mouth. Another Kändler group, this time of Scaramouche and Columbine, was sold in 1961 for £800.

Henri Deux ware, fine pottery which once enjoyed a great reputation, was made in France at the time of Henry

II and of Diana of Poitiers. The period was the middle of the 16th century, and only a few score pieces survive. In the Hamilton sale of 1882 a cup 4 in. high of this ware sold for £1,218, and even a salt-cellar brought £840. These prices were not the limit, however, for at a Fountaine sale two years later a candlestick 12¾ in. high fetched £3,675. Considering the change in the value of money that has taken place since, these are impressive figures, for we should have to multiply them a few times to find to-day's equivalent. But what would the prices have been a few years before or a few years after these particular sales? There are fashions in antique pottery and porcelain of little intrinsic merit, and sometimes competition at auctions can become a somewhat expensive pastime for the uninitiated.

Sèvres porcelain is held in high regard and sells well in spite of numerous pieces being available. A Sèvres yellow-ground part dinner and dessert service fetched £520 at Sotheby's in 1956. The decoration consisted of a spray of roses in the centre, garlanded with roses entwined with a blue ribbon on a broad yellow band. Such a colour scheme is a bit gaudy, but boldness can be very effective, as some of our own contemporary pottery shows. This particular service dated from about the year 1795.

Anton's Antiques

At its highest level, antique porcelain sells at prices which seem staggering to the layman. Towards the end of 1954, nine small figure subjects by Anton Bustelli were sold at Christie's for £35,647. They were made at the Nymphenburg factory between 1754 and 1763, and represented the stock figures of Italian comedy. The subjects became very popular because companies of Italian players used to tour the Continent and gained great esteem.

Perhaps even more impressive than the total sum realised, were the amounts paid for individual items. Of the set being dispersed, the figures of Harlequin and Lalage brought 10,600 guineas for the pair, this record sum paid by S. Rosenberg of London and New York. Julia went for 4,600 guineas and Corine for 4,200 guineas. The Victoria and Albert Museum was able to secure only Columbine, and the price paid was a comparatively modest 2,500 guineas.

The Orient

Chinese pieces are very modestly priced considering their age and beauty, and may well become much more valuable when their merits are fully appreciated. It is, however, necessary to distinguish between the superb specimens of the finest periods, and the greatly inferior later work when things had become commercialised. Comparatively few examples of Chinese porcelain are offered in London, but a good many in Paris: the French, in fact, appreciate Oriental art and understand it.

The superbly decorative T'ang horses only fetch modest prices compared with many pieces of much less artistic merit. In November, 1950, a Bactrian prancing horse, 10 in. high on a wooden stand, went for £52, a glazed saddled horse, 28 in. high, for £50, and another prancing horse in red-tinted unglazed pottery for £60, all at Sotheby's.

It is sometimes claimed that to buy works of art can prove a profitable investment. Certainly the pleasure to be derived from the possession of, say, fine porcelain can pay rich dividends to proud owners, although not in the form of cash. Capital appreciation is often disappointing when considered dispassionately. To quote an example, a pair of Chinese enamelled porcelain vases was sold for 660 guineas in 1938 and resold for 950 guineas in 1956. Although these were attractive works in powder-blue, $17\frac{1}{4}$ in. high, with brilliantly ornamented panels with finches perched on branches of prunus and magnolia in bloom, the pieces were fairly late and not of a specially rare type, or the rise in value might have been greater. Nevertheless, an appreciation of 45 per cent in a period during which money shrank to one-third its value was far from keeping pace with the circumstances.

In another case two Chinese tea bowls and saucers, which had been sold at Christie's in 1938 for 320 guineas, were sold there again in 1956 for 600 guineas. Although diminutive in scale these had the austere beauty of the *famille noire* to which they belonged. Internally they had panels of black, aubergine, yellow and green on which were painted flower sprays, while externally the enamel was black painted with prunus branches in white, aubergine and green.

On the other hand capital appreciation can sometimes be very rapid. In 1950 a pair of Oriental porcelain cranes, dating from the 18th century, were disposed of from the collection of Lady Nairne. When put up for auction at Sotheby's they brought £480, which did not seem by any means a negligible figure. A similar pair, enamelled in blue, puce, white, black and red, 17 in. high, offered in the same rooms in 1956, brought £1,300.

It would be taking cupidity to extremes to expect this to happen regularly in the hazardous field of works of art, though it does happen not infrequently, and is then a very pleasant surprise for the owners.

A very interesting sale of Chinese porcelain took place at Christie's in May, 1956, when a comparatively small collection sold for £31,370. One of the features of the occasion was a departure from the rather dismal present-day ritual of treasures that have been domiciled in Europe being bought for export to the United States. Instead the sale was on behalf of American interests and some of the most spirited bidding came from Holland. The prestige which London had enjoyed as an art mart for more than a century and a half was emphasised once more.

At this particular sale the items were of the 17th and 18th centuries and included some examples of the splendidly colourful figures of Chinese mounted warriors. One pair of these horsemen, 8¼ in. high, in aubergine, black, green, white and yellow, went for 4,200 guineas, and other single figures of this type secured 1,000 and 1,300 guineas apiece. A total of over £6,800 for four pieces seems adequate payment even in these days of depreciated values, especially as the modelling was not quite of the same excellence as the colouring.

Prices of Oriental ceramics in particular continue to make remarkable progress, so that in 1961 at Christie's a pair of Ch'ien Lung hawks were sold for £7,560, while at Sotheby's a pair of pheasants, 13¾ in. high and of the same period, went for the record price of £8,800.

In 1962 a pair of 14th century Ming dishes, one blue and white, the other copper-red, brought £2,700, and a 13 in. wine ewer of this period £8,800—an impressive price for a single piece. Three other Ming specimens, an underglazed blue and yellow dish, a globular jar and a green dragon bowl, went together for £9,300.

14

GLOSSARY

Albastros
A type of diminutive Greek oil jar with two small ears by which it can be suspended.

Amatorii
Pottery plaques made at Pesaro in Italy for presentation by young men to their betrothed. They bore the name of the lady with some complimentary adjective, "Camilla bella," "Lucretia diva," or the like.

Amphorae
Two-handled Greek jars for holding wine, oil or other liquids. They were often of large size.

Angouleme
A hard-porcelain factory in Paris, founded about 1780, of which the Duc d'Angouleme was patron. The name is also applied to the products of the works.

Barbotine
A method of decorating china figures with a fine ceramic network closely resembling lace.

Basalt
A black porcelain first used by Wedgwood, from an African name for a kind of bluish-black rock.

Bear Jugs
Jugs in the shape of a bear with a removable head that could be used as a cup. These were made at Nottingham throughout the 18th century, being coated with rough scraps of clay of a reddish-brown colour to resemble fur.

Bellarmine
A large jug made in the form of a short, rotund, bearded man with harsh, coarse features. Made at Cologne and in Holland as a biting burlesque on Cardinal Bellermine (d. 1621), who had made himself hateful to the Protestants by his opposition to the

reformed religion. Bellarmines were afterwards made at Fulham.
(*See* GREYBEARD.)

Belleek
A fine glazed Parian body treated with metallic lustres.

Bird Tureens
Tureens in the form of fowls such as ducks and turkeys, made
in porcelain at Meissen and afterwards at Chelsea.

Bishop Bowls
Bowls shaped like a mitre, and used for serving a kind of punch
known as "bishop" (made of port wine, oranges or lemons, and
sugar) popular in Scandinavian countries.

Bisque
A type of unglazed white porcelain commonly used for making
statuettes.

Black Ware
This ware was made in England from the 17th century, and was
brought to perfection by Wedgwood. For a period jet teapots
enjoyed great popularity.

Blanc-de-Chine
The name given to a kind of white porcelain imported into
Europe in the 18th century from the Chinese province of
Fuchien. It often has a relief pattern of sprays of plum-
blossom.

Bocage
The background of flowers and foliage attached to porcelain
figures, which besides being a decorative feature serves to
support the figures while in the kiln.

Boccaleri
A guild of potters active in Venice from the mid-15th to the
mid-17th centuries.

Bone Ash
Calcined bones of cattle, largely used in English china.

Bone China
British bone china is the equivalent of Continental porcelain,
but is distinguished by its exceptional strength, whiteness and
translucency.

Bottle Oven
Early kilns in the Potteries derived their traditional name from
being shaped like a medieval wine-bottle.

Buccaros
Scented Mexican pottery brought to Europe by the Portuguese, and afterwards copied here.

Caffaggiola
A type of Tuscan ware that followed the Della Robbia tradition; characterised by a very pure white enamel and one of brilliant cobalt blue.

Canettes
Jugs of rough stoneware with fluted decoration first made in Bavaria in the 15th century.

Capo di Monte
Fine Italian porcelain made in the 18th and early 19th centuries, and often imitated since. The name is also given to the factory where this porcelain was produced from 1736.

Celadon
The name given in France to some of the first Chinese porcelain to be imported into Europe, of a beautiful sea-green colour.

Ceramics
A general term for the potter's art and for pottery itself. From the Greek *keramos*, potter's earth, and hence pottery. One of the earliest uses of pottery was for the making of drinking cups and perhaps for this reason it came about that Keramos, the son of Bacchus and Ariadne, was the patron of potters.

Chervettes
Pharmacy jugs with a short neck and wide spout, for holding oils and syrups.

China
Porcelain ware, originally imported from China. Now often applied loosely to crockery in general.

China Clay
A fine white clay used for making porcelain, employed in China from about the second century B.C. In Britain its use was introduced in Cornwall by Cookworthy in 1755.

Chu Ware
Figures and other objects made by the famous Chinese ceramic artists *Chu-ong* (the venerable Chu) and his daughter *Chu-kiao* (the pretty Chu).

Costrels
Oval flattened bottles with loops through which leather thongs

could be placed. They were carried by monks and pilgrims from
the 13th to 16th centuries.

Crackle
Crazing of the glaze, used by the Chinese from about the 10th
century A.D. as a form of decoration.

Crock
An old word of wide application used for any kind of coarse
earthenware vessel, such as a pot, jar or pitcher.

Crockery
The general term for fired earthenware, in contrast to china or
earthenware.

Cyathus
An ancient Greek measuring cup or ladle.

Damas Ware
Pottery made in Damascus from the 16th century onwards,
having a greyish white base richly decorated with such flowers
as tulips, carnations and roses in blue, turquoise and other
striking colours.

Delft Pottery
Decorated earthenware was made at Delft in Holland from the
16th to 18th centuries. The same type of pottery, using the same
name, was afterwards produced at a number of English centres,
including Lambeth and Bristol.

Dog of Fo
The ugly and fantastic monster forming a lid-grip or handle on
certain types of Oriental pottery. The creature was a guardian
of Buddhist temples.

Earthenware
The term is applied broadly to most types of pottery that are
not translucent.

Eggshell China
Porcelain of exceptional thinness first made in China about 1410.

Enamel
This term is used in contradistinction to glaze as indicating a
material rendered opaque by tin or the like, so that when applied
to pots the body base is hidden.

Encaustic Painting
A method of decorating invented by Josiah Wedgwood, in
imitation of Etruscan and Roman earthenware.

Faience
A kind of fine pottery with painted decoration originally made at the town of Faenza in Italy.

Figuline
An earthen vessel, from the Latin *figulinus*, a potter.

Flashed Glaze
A technique perfected by the Chinese and producing special colour effects, such as blues splashed with spots of red and lilac.

Frog Mugs
Mugs made in Leeds and Newcastle-on-Tyne with a model of a frog inside which became visible only when part of the contents had been drunk.

Glaze
A transparent coating given to pottery from a very early date to protect it. Glazes were used on pottery in Assyria, Babylon and Egypt.

Glost
The glost firing is that carried out at a comparatively low temperature to fix the glaze on pottery which has already been burnt once. In this way the pots are made "glossy."

Greybeard
A stoneware jar for liquor, bearing a little mask of a bearded man. In the reign of Queen Elizabeth I this kind of container was imported from the Rhineland and copied by Dutch potters who had settled in Britain to escape religious persecution. (*See* BELLARMINE.)

Hard Porcelain
Also known as true porcelain, and consisting of china clay, feldspar and silica, fired to a high temperature. (*See* SOFT PORCELAIN.)

Hochst Ware
China made at Hochst, in Germany, during the 18th century.

Honorific Marks
Symbols used on Chinese porcelain to show for whom it was made.

Hydrea
A kind of Greek water pitcher having a main handle and two side ones.

Ibis Mummy Pots
Conical vessels of red clay with convex lids, used by the early Egyptians for holding the embalmed body of the sacred bird.

Ironstone
A very hard type of earthenware patented by Mason of Fenton in 1813 and used for decorative purposes.

Jasper
The name given by Josiah Wedgwood to a body composition of carbonate and sulphate of baryta mixed with flint and clay stained with cobalt oxide. The colouring was not merely on the surface, as in other pottery, but was uniform throughout the body.

Jet
A brilliant black ware used for teapots, jugs and the like, made from a red body with a blue glaze.

Jewelled Porcelain
Decorative pieces made at Sèvres were sometimes enriched by the introduction of small pieces of coloured glass to imitate jewels. English manufacturers made the same kind of thing with enamels substituted for glass.

Jumbo Cup
An extra large cup or magnum, with a bowl-shaped body.

Krater
An ancient Greek vessel for heating water and for other purposes.

Lead Glaze
Lead has been used in glazes since the days of ancient Babylon, and was long the only known way of glazing soft pottery.

Majolica
A kind of pottery having a red or grey base covered by fine opaque white enamel containing a high proportion of tin. First made many centuries ago in the island of Majorca, but afterwards a common product in Italy and among the Arabs and Saracens.

Mocha Cup
A coffee cup of small size, named after a choice quality of coffee originally obtained from Mocha, a fortified seaport in south-west Arabia.

152

Music Plates
Delft and other dessert plates bearing the music of a song to be sung at the end of a meal.

Oinochoe
An elegant style of jug used in ancient Greece for serving wine at table. The word is from the Greek *oinos*, wine.

On-Glaze
This term is used for the kind of decoration applied on top of the fired glaze. To fix the colours the ware has to be fired again in an enamel or decorating kiln. (*See* UNDER-GLAZE.)

Parian
The name of a body composition consisting of three-fifths chinastone and two-fifths feldspar. It is used for busts and statuettes, and being non-plastic has to be formed by casting or coulage. Its name was adopted because the ware resembles Parian marble, from Paros, an isle in the Ægean Sea.

Pastillage
Decoration by pouring a thin stream of coloured slip on to pottery. The process was introduced near Beauvais in the 15th century.

Pâte-sur-Pâte
The application of successive layers of thin slip for decorative purposes.

Pelike
An old Greek name for a wide-bellied type of amphora.

Petuntse
A feldspathic rock used in making porcelain. It is also known as Cornish stone. The word is an 18th century phonetic French rendering of the Chinese *pai-tun-tzŭ*, meaning little white brick.

Pig
The Scottish word for an earthenware crock, a hot-water bottle or other vessel.

Porcelain
A kind of pottery which is strong, thin, white, highly vitrified and semi-transparent. The term is largely confined to Continental products, the English equivalent being bone china.

The word has a picturesque origin, coming from *porcellana*, the Italian for the shell of Venus, and ultimately from a diminutive of the Latin *porco, porcus*, a hog, because of the resemblance of the shell to a hog's back.

Pot
The first pots were used for drinking. The word itself is from the Greek *potos*, drinking. The original meaning has remained with very little change in such related words as *potations*, a term for tippling; *poteen*, Irish whisky illicitly distilled; and *potion*, a dose of medicine.

Another related word is *pottle*, a liquid measure of four pints, or alternatively a large tankard. " Pottle-deep," incidentally, means to the bottom of the tankard.

Pottern
A term indicating relationship to potters or pottery. Pottern-ore is an ore vitrifying with heat and used to glaze pottery.

Pottery
The term pottery, like the French *poterie*, applies to all ceramic vessels, including those made from porcelain. The three main divisions of pottery are earthenware, stoneware and china or porcelain. The word is also used for any factory in which ceramics are made. " The Potteries" is the region in Stafford-shire centred upon the city of Stoke-on-Trent, where the bulk of English pottery of every description is manufactured.

Pot-Waller
A man engaged in pot-walloping. Before the Reform Bill of 1832, one was able to qualify as a voter in certain English boroughs by boiling a pot on one's own fireplace within the borough. Sometimes a bogus claim was established by a man boiling a pot in the open air before witnesses. The word is derived from pot with the addition of the old English *wallan*, to boil.

Quodlibetz
Literally "what you will." A term applied to the random or haphazard distribution of decoration on Copenhagen porcelain of the 18th century.

Replacer
A piece made specially to replace one lost or broken from a valuable old service.

Saggar
A fireclay box in which delicate porcelain was placed while in the kiln. The saggar protected its contents from direct contact with the flame during firing. The word is believed to be a corruption of "safeguard."

Scale Pattern
A form of decoration in blue and green, closely resembling overlapping fish-scales, used on Turkish pottery in the 16th century. Worcester scale-blue is a related type of design adopted there in the latter half of the 18th century.

Sgraffito
Decoration cut with a pointed instrument through a coating of white slip.

Slip
Clay in a state of liquid suspension, or a creamy paste for coating and decorating pottery. The word is related to *slime* and *slipslop*.

Soft Porcelain
Also called "semi-porcelain." The name sometimes given to early types of Western porcelain made before all the secrets of true porcelain had been discovered. In porcelain the proportion of fluxes is high, so that it can be fired at a relatively low temperature. (*See* HARD PORCELAIN.)

Sprigging
Sprigged decoration was clay moulded in the form of flowers and foliage, and attached by slip to stoneware or earthenware.

Stamnos
An ancient Greek short-necked wine storage jar.

Stippling
A mottled type of colour decoration obtained with brushes or sponges.

Stoneware
Pottery made from clay and flint or hard siliceous clay. It has a dense and impervious body, and is usually of a cream or brown colour because of the iron oxide present.

Terracotta
The word means literally "baked earth." Brownish-orange pottery which is not glazed. It is more porous than earthenware, and the firing temperature is lower. The term also covers a statuette or other object of art made from a composition of clay and sand hardened by fire.

Terrine
An earthenware jar to hold some table delicacy. The word is from the Latin *terra*, the earth. (*See* TUREEN.)

Tortoiseshell Ware
Staffordshire earthenware which has been given a mottled appearance by the use of a manganese brown glaze.

Tureen
A deep covered vessel for holding soup, originally made of earthenware. (*See* TERRINE.)

Under-Glaze
The type of decoration applied to pottery before it is glazed. An under-glaze colour comprises a stain and also a flux which helps the colour to penetrate the pottery body. (*See* ON-GLAZE.)

Willow Pattern
This most famous of all patterns for decorating domestic china was adapted from a Chinese design. Said to have been first engraved by Thomas Minton, during his apprenticeship at the Caughley China Works.

Index

157